DOCTOR'S ORDERS

When Elma W. Bagg's husband was ordered by a doctor to eliminate salt from his diet, Mrs. Bagg resolved not to let that order become a life sentence to bland, tasteless food. **COOKING WITHOUT A GRAIN OF SALT** is the happy result of her efforts to produce appetizing, palatable dishes with imaginative use of herbs, condiments, wine, and sheer inspiration.

Not only does this book present the most comprehensive collection of low-sodium recipes, it also offers hundreds of sprightly and encouraging suggestions for maintaining prescribed sodium levels while traveling, dining out, and visiting friends.

The author's friendly and personable style combines with a wealth of imaginative recipes to make this book a boon to the housewife suddenly confronted with the prospect of preparing appetizing meals—from take-along lunches to party canapés—without the use of salt.

THE ARITHRITIC'S COOKBOOK by Collin Dong &
   Jane Banks
THE ART OF JEWISH COOKING by Jennie Grossinger
BEST RECIPES FROM THE BACKS OF BOXES,
   BOTTLES, CANS AND JARS by Cecil Dyer
BETTER HOMES AND GARDENS ALL-TIME
   FAVORITE CASSEROLE RECIPES
BETTER HOMES AND GARDENS NEW COOKBOOK
   (All new edition)
BLEND IT SPLENDID: THE NATURAL FOODS
   BLENDER BOOK by Stan and Floss Dworkin
COOKING WITH HERBS AND SPICES
   by Craig Claiborne
CREPE COOKERY by Mable Hoffman
CROCKERY COOKERY by Mable Hoffman
THE FRENCH CHEF COOKBOOK by Julia Child
JUEL ANDERSEN'S TOFU KITCHEN
   by Juel Andersen
KATHY COOKS NATURALLY by Kathy Hoshijo
LAUREL'S KITCHEN by Laurel Robertson,
   Carol Flinders and Bronwen Godfrey
MADAME WU'S ART OF CHINESE COOKING
   by Sylvia Wu
THE LOW BLOOD SUGAR COOKBOOK
   by Francyne Davis
MAKE-A-MIX COOKERY by Nevada Harward,
   Madeline Westover and Karine Eliason
MASTERING MICROWAVE COOKING
   by Maria Luisa Scott and Jack Denton Scott
MORE-WITH-LESS COOKBOOK by Doris Longacre
MOTHER WONDERFUL'S CHEESECAKES AND
   OTHER GOODIES by Myra Chanin
THE OLD-FASHIONED RECIPE BOOK by Carla Emery
PUTTING FOOD BY by Ruth Hertzberg,
   Beatrice Vaughan and Janet Greene
RICHARD DEACON'S MICROWAVE COOKERY
THE ROMAGNOLIS' TABLE by Margaret and
   G. Franco Romagnoli
SOURDOUGH COOKERY by Rita Davenport

Cooking Without a Grain of Salt

By Elma W. Bagg

Foreword by A. Gregory Jameson, M.D.

BANTAM BOOKS
TORONTO   NEW YORK   LONDON · SYDNEY

COOKING WITHOUT A GRAIN OF SALT

*A Bantam Book / published by arrangement with
Doubleday & Company, Inc.*

PRINTING HISTORY

Doubleday edition published May 1964

2nd printing .... June 1964	5th printing .. December 1967
3rd printing .... May 1965	6th printing .... June 1969
4th printing .... August 1966	7th printing .... April 1970
8th printing .... February 1971	

Bantam edition / February 1972

2nd printing .. December 1972	7th printing .... June 1977
3rd printing .... June 1973	8th printing .... March 1978
4th printing .. November 1974	9th printing .... March 1979
5th printing .... February 1976	10th printing .... July 1979
6th printing .... July 1976	11th printing .... May 1980
12th printing ....February 1981	

ISBN 0–553–20076–3

Published simultaneously in the United States and Canada

Bantam Books are published by Bantam Books, Inc. Its trademark, consisting of the words "Bantam Books" and the por-
trayal of a bantam is Registered in U.S. Patent and Trademark
Office and in other countries. Marca Registrada. Bantam
Books, Inc., 666 Fifth Avenue, New York, New York 10103.

PRINTED IN THE UNITED STATES OF AMERICA

21 20 19 18 17 16 15

To My Husband, Ted,
Who Made this Book Necessary
and
to His Doctor, Alfred E. Gras, M.D.
Who Demanded That Ted's "Necessary"
Be Very Necessary

Foreword

Diets with reduced salt content have, for a number of years, been part of the treatment of various illnesses involving the heart, blood vessels, or other organ systems. Such low-sodium diets and salt-free diets are important and effective components of the over-all treatment. Traditionally, they exhibit one severe drawback, a general lack of palatability. They tend to be flat and tasteless.

The problem of producing a palatable, tasty diet has not received its due. Too many patients have been forced to choose between sticking to a diet so unpalatable that they lose their interest in food and cheat, using salt in excess of their doctor's orders, to their detriment. While the problem is difficult in one's own home, sticking to a special sodium-restricted diet when traveling, visiting, or eating out may be well-nigh impossible.

Mrs. Bagg's book, inspired by her wish to improve her husband's lot after he was put on a low-sodium diet, goes a long way toward solving these problems. Her recipes, carefully checked for sodium content, are made enjoyable and appetizing by a skillful use of herbs, condiments, and wine. Their large number allows a more than adequate variety of menus. Her meat dishes are well chosen and appealing, but her vegetable recipes are particularly noteworthy when compared with the mashed and boiled affairs usually served as part of a low-salt diet. Her suggestions for handling the problems of obtaining a proper diet while traveling, eating out, or visiting will prove helpful to many.

Anyone having to live on a low-sodium diet, or having to plan meals for someone who is, will find this book a great boon. Mrs. Bagg's care and skill in working out and assembling such a wide variety of recipes has resulted in a book for which every "unsalty," as she calls them, can be grateful.

As Mrs. Bagg is careful to emphasize, before adopting these recipes, check with your own doctor.

A. Gregory Jameson, M.D.
Director, Cardiovascular Laboratory,
The Presbyterian Hospital,
New York City

Contents

Recipes mentioned in the text and follow by an asterisk may be found by consulting the index.

Introduction

This book began as a record for myself. Now it is a joy to be able to share these "notes" with you. It all came about because of the need to cook delicious meals without a grain of salt.

Most "notes" have many reasons for being written. Mine had two: first, the love for my husband; and second, the hope that they might have the same result for others who are obliged to be on a low-sodium diet. By result, I do not mean medical. This was not up to me. It was up to me, however, to accept the challenge that it was possible to prepare appetizing, tasty meals without the use of salt. My first goal was to make my husband contented and satisfied at mealtime. Otherwise this low-sodium diet would fail.

In the beginning, our doctor, who likes to ski in Vermont as well as practice medicine, was kind and at the same time stern, explaining the program he demanded should be followed to the T. I was given food lists to study. They showed what was permitted and forbidden. I was also told the number of milligrams of sodium my husband was to have each day. In my confused state of mind I gathered from the diet lists that one could eat rice (unsalted, how awful) but couldn't eat beets, spinach, and celery. What was wrong with beets, spinach, and celery? I always told my children to eat them. I had no idea what sodium content or a milligram was. I have learned.

The first dinner I used ten pans. Ted's meal was awful. Our lovely country kitchen was a mess. The fire in the kitchen hearth didn't even cheer me. Poor Ted and that horrible, dry rice. I thought we'd never have cheerful family meals again. It was after this shambles that I vowed to make our meals as nutritious and attractive as ever and at the same time strictly adhere to the diet.

Thank goodness that I had always been interested in herb cookery and most herbs are very low in sodium. Salt is not the only seasoning. Salt appeals to one's sense of taste but not very much to the sense of smell. Go smell some. The sense of smell is most important in our desire to eat. The aroma of delicate herbs and wines in unsalted food makes unsalty forget that the now forbidden salt was once a part of his life.

My first job was to use old, favorite recipes, and by eliminating the salt and substituting herbs, a little wine, vinegar, or lemon I created tasty dishes. This was trial and error. Sometimes things worked well the first time, sometimes not so well, requiring continued experimentation. I have always liked to collect recipes. This was a big help, and gradually I was able to develop a number of recipes that worked well.

I had the most trouble with the technicalities of the gram, milligram, and sodium content. The first time I looked up gram in the dictionary, I found the wrong gram, a "chick pea found in the East Indies." The gram I was after was a "fundamental unit of mass." Why couldn't it be the first one? In our lay language I found that a gram is a "unit of weight in the metric system." I decided not to worry about the word "metric" and promptly forgot it. I did remember that there are 28 grams in an ounce. That was simple. I found that if you divided one gram into 1000 parts you have a milligram. (Don't worry about this, either.) Later when I decided to write this book, I determined, as I found in the beginning it was easier, to list the milligrams as measured in teaspoons, tablespoons, and cupfuls in most familiar foods.

I learned early to READ LABELS. This I think you should underline in RED INK.

As I studied I found that sodium is a mineral basic and necessary to animal and plant life, and that salt (sodium chloride) is a compound that has been used in seasoning from time immemorial. In one tablespoon of salt there are 6800 milligrams of sodium. In comparison, one tablespoon of sugar contains a negligible amount of sodium.

I also learned early how to manage when going to a restaurant. Our first evening out was a great success; Ted felt better and so did I. I bought a small insulated bag and a great, huge pocketbook. Thank goodness they were the style. I took Ted's low-sodium margarine, crackers, bread, even a piece of parsley (these we called "the sneak-ins"). We were going to make this fun. Grapefruit, lamb chops, baked potato, lettuce and tomato salad with olive oil, vinegar, and granulated sugar were ordered. I think we told the waitress four times, maybe six, not to have the chef salt the chop (we have learned since that chefs rarely salt chops). I think Ted had grapefruit again for dessert.

We have had wonderful co-operation from hotels and clubs where large luncheons and dinners were to be served. The dining-room manager was called, and the lamb chop, baked potato, and salad were always at the proper place. The manager's only request was to have my husband identify himself to the headwaiter. Can't you imagine how the meat-and-potato man sitting across the table eating creamed chicken in a patty shell envied my husband?

When summer came we wanted to have weekends in Massachusetts to visit our daughter and son-in-law, Susan and Richard Todd and their dear Emily and also son Bob and his wife Sally and their wonderful children Ted, Chris, Jonathan, Hazzy and Melissa. As part of our traveling equipment, because low-sodium bread and margarine need refrigeration, we bought a car icebox. Picnics are fun in New England, and eat-out dinners are not a problem. Some fine day that ice box is going to Europe.

Cooking Without a Grain of Salt will only be deeply gratifying to me if it fulfills in some small degree its intent —to make a sodium-restricted diet a happy chapter in a family's life.

The recipes in this book have been tested and retested and are created so that only a salt shaker need be put before our salty[1] friends. Ten pans won't be needed. Unsalty will like them and so will salty.

---

[1] For easy reference, I have named the sodium-restricted dieter "unsalty" and the person without a sodium restriction "salty."

Cooking
Without
a Grain
of Salt

1 For Salty and Unsalty, Who Read This Book and Use These Recipes

First to Salty

You are not on this diet. So don't try being your own doctor and start experimenting with your intake of sodium. These recipes were designed for a family in whose midst a member is on a sodium-restricted diet. Buy your own bread, butter, and mayonnaise, and eat all the pickles, olives, and ham you want. In fact, with the whole untouchable list that follows, just go haywire. I do. You should see my lunches sometimes, with all the high-sodiums. Seriously, though, we should recognize the fact that sodium is one of the nutrients that we can eat in too large amounts.

When you have people in for meals, explain to your guests that the food was prepared and cooked without the use of salt. Your own family-circle salties are already aware of the omission of salt. Fill the salt shaker up to the top and place it close to your or their plates. Always place on the table all the relishes and breads that salty loves so dearly.

Salt is the main source of sodium in the food we eat. In other words, a large proportion of our daily intake of sodium comes from the salt we add to our food—whether it be you or someone else who put it there.

The recipes in this book are so tasty that many times I have made myself use salt, because I think I should.

Happy salting to you!

1

Now to Unsalty

Just because you feel so much better don't try and convince everyone you meet to go on a low-sodium diet. This diet was ordered for *you* by *your* doctor. The "everyone you meet" has his own doctor and his own ailments.

Your doctor will determine the amount of sodium-restriction for *your* diet. The milligrams may be strictly counted each day or you may be given a list showing foods that are permitted and those that are forbidden. Do as he says. All right?

Good Health and Happiness to You.

2   Listen Carefully

The recipes in *Cooking Without a Grain of Salt* were created primarily for a sodium-restricted diet of 500 milligrams per day (in 24 hours). To insure well-balanced meals, careful planning will be needed for 500 milligrams, but if your sodium restriction is under 500 milligrams, very careful planning must be employed. In order for you to secure an adequate amount of calcium when your sodium restriction is between 200 and 400 milligrams of sodium, the use of low-sodium milk will be necessary. There are 122 milligrams of sodium in 8 ounces (1 cup) of whole milk but in the same amount of low-sodium milk (reconstituted) there are only 7 milligrams.

If your diet permits more than 500 milligrams per day, these recipes are adaptable. Your doctor may allow *light* salting in the cooking or in the preparation of food, or, if the food was prepared without salt, a *limited* amount may be permitted at the table. Remember, there are 570 milligrams of sodium in ¼ of a teaspoon of salt. So if the limit is ¼ of a teaspoon, that *is* the limit. No more. You must understand this.

If there are foods on the following "touchable" lists or ingredients in these recipes that your doctor forbids, obey his orders and do not use those foods. On the other hand, he may allow some foods that are on the "untouchable" lists.

Your doctor knows your individual needs. The only way a doctor can truly assist and benefit your health is for you, unsalty, to abide by his instructions. Please listen to him carefully.

3

3 To Hospital Unsalty

My small bit, during the war, was to be a nurse's aide in our local hospital. This was my first experience with low-sodium diets and the people who were on them. The patients did much complaining, and I remember feeling sorry about their plight. Don't you, hospital unsalty, for one minute feel a bit sorry for yourself. Just be thankful and happy that you have a doctor who will help and guide you back to health. You help yourself too. I will tell you about "secret hospital sneak-ins." Give this list to your doctor and ask him if it is all right. I think he will say yes.

Ask your hospital sitter (you know, the member of the family who comes every day to sit with you and to cheer you) to fill twelve shakers (formerly known as salt shakers) with allspice, curry, dill, dry mustard, garlic powder, mace, mint, nutmeg, onion powder, oregano, paprika, and sage. You can buy shakers in the five-and-ten in colors to match your home kitchen.

Keep fresh lemons, a small bottle of vinegar, low-sodium dietetic catsup, and chili sauce right by your side. There are only 0.7 mg. of sodium in a tablespoon of this kind of catsup or chili sauce. The rest of the herbs and seasonables on this list you don't have to count.

Now do your own experimenting. Lemon juice and vinegar are good with so many foods. Do something different at every meal. Read over the recipes in the rest of the book and plan your meals for your first day home. You can learn to count your own milligrams and calories, too, if your doctor says you must. Get your hospital sitter to buy a little notebook for you to figure your milligrams and also

4

to jot down your combinations of herbs and seasonables that taste good to you. Your hospital sitter doesn't like to go empty-handed to the hospital.

I salute you, hospital unsalty, because I know you have courage. Take care.

Here Is Your List of Herbs and the Foods They Complement

ALLSPICE

Applesauce
Cranberry sauce
Fruit

Gravies
Meat

CURRY

Eggs
Fish
Lamb

Mayonnaise
Veal

DILL

(ground)

Beef
Cabbage
Carrots
Cauliflower
Chicken
Cucumber
Fish
Green beans

Lamb
Macaroni
Potato
Potato salad
Sour cream
Tomato juice
Tomato soup

DRY MUSTARD

Asparagus
Broccoli
Brussels sprouts
Cabbage
Chicken

Fish
Mayonnaise
Meat
Potatoes

GARLIC POWDER

(not garlic salt)

Fish
Meat
Potatoes

Vegetables
Vegetable salads

MACE

Apples (fresh or baked)
Carrots
Cauliflower
Fruit salad

Lamb chops
Potatoes
Squash
Veal chops

MINT

Carrots
Fruit
Fruit juice

Hot or iced tea
Lamb
Peas

NUTMEG

Chicken
Fish
Hot lemonade
Meat loaf

Potatoes
Puddings
Toast or bread
Veal

ONION POWDER
(not onion salt)

Meat dishes
Potatoes

Soup
Stews

OREGANO

Eggplant
Hamburgers

Tomatoes
Vegetable salads

PAPRIKA

Chicken
Fish
Meat

Potatoes
Salad dressings

SAGE

Eggs
Fish
Lima beans

Onions
Pork chops
Tomatoes

4 Unsalty's Eat-Out Breakfasts

Only once did unsalty's eat-out breakfast present a problem. It occurred on Easter Sunday and had to do with an egg. We had car trouble and were delayed a day arriving home. This is a lesson to you. Always take more bread in the sneak-in bag than you think you will use. Our sneak-in bag was empty, but we didn't think it would be a problem. There was always fruit or fruit juice, an egg or shredded wheat, and coffee.

However, in the restaurant where we had Easter breakfast there wasn't any shredded wheat. The waiter said they didn't boil eggs. My husband said—so amiably, that he thought the chef wouldn't mind—"Just tell him to put the egg in a pan with water and boil it for three minutes." Off the waiter went and back he came. Nope, they couldn't change their rules. Their other eggs were fried and scrambled in bacon grease. They did have coffee.

This truly was the only time that our fellow Americans weren't more than anxious to please. I looked out the window and saw people, in this lovely little country town, going to church. They had fine faces.

5 Unsalty's Eat-Out Lunches

Lunches for our working unsalty can be a problem. Don't make them a problem. Pack a lunch—not even the neighbor on the bus or train will know. (You can see we live in suburbia.) Put the choice morsels in an insulated bag—then—here is the trick—save status paper bags from Altman, Bonwit, Brooks Brothers, etc. Shove the whole lunch inside. The status bag can be used over and over again. Another way is to get very friendly at your lunch counter or wherever you ate when you were salty. My husband did, and the lunch problem was solved—until the lunch counter closed. Then we took up the status bags. When we were on the "in," low-sodium bread, crackers, margarine, peanut butter, and cheese plus honey and jelly were sent along every week to be placed in the lunch-counter icebox. A salad with oil and vinegar dressing and fruits would be served. Ted always paid for the sandwich even though he had already paid for it—tipped too! Oh well, most things now cost twice what they're worth and they aren't always worth it. This service was.

6   Bill of Fare for Unsalty's Eat-Out Dinner

THE FIRST TICKLE OF THE PALATE

Apple juice
Avocado (sliced)
Cantaloupe
Cranberry juice

Grapefruit
Grapefruit juice
Honeydew melon
Pineapple juice

THE SECOND TICKLE OF THE PALATE

NO SOUP (loaded with sodium)

More of the first tickle of the palate if you wish to be
sociable

THE MAIN SUSTENANCE
(COOKED WEIGHT)

3 oz. center-cut roast beef
3 oz. breast of chicken
3 oz. fresh fish
3 oz. lamb chop

3 oz. pork chop
3 oz. steak
3 oz. turkey

Baked potato with 2 teaspoons unsalted butter or
margarine

THE SNEAK-INS

Low-sodium bread or crackers

Unsalted butter or low-sodium margarine with parsley!

NO VEGETABLES. They, too, could be loaded

Green salad with tomato, oil, vinegar, and granulated-sugar dressing. Unsalty, pour on what you want. REMEMBER NO CELERY. If chef puts it in you take it out

DESSERT

More of the first and second tickle of the palate
You could add blueberries or peaches—watch the cream or milk

DRINKABLES

Coffee   Sanka   Tea

Or Whatever your doctor or mother taught you. Now stick to this. If unsalty was served two chops you can use the sneak-in bag for a sneak-out bag and put the second chop in the status bag for tomorrow's lunch.

A Note to Maître d'

When unsalty is your guest you can be most helpful. Always have a tray available holding a decanter of oil and vinegar with a few herb shakers filled with basil, dill, nutmeg, oregano, and mint. Do reserve a corner of the freezer for unsalted bread, butter, and margarine. You will render a real service to your fellow man and a generous "donation" to our heart associations.

7 When Your Friends Have the Latchstring Out

News could travel on how difficult it is to cook for some-one on a low-sodium diet. When you are invited out for dinner don't bother explaining about diet, just remember your teachings and say thank you. Now take out your friend the insulated bag. Put the regular sneak-ins, low-sodium margarine, bread and crackers, in the bottom. Add a lamb chop sprinkled with ginger, a foil-wrapped potato, and go to have fun. Just stick the potato and chop in the oven when you arrive. There should always be room for a bit more. This performance is easier on the hostess. She, and rightfully so, should be able to try out her favorite company recipes and the glamorous dessert pic-tured in a "home" magazine—but this is not for unsalty.

Of course, your hostess may wish to plan her menu around unsalty. Then be gracious again, and say, "Thank you so very much."

8 When You Go Abroad

Don't worry when you leave these shores. Copy this list, buy some canned low-sodium bread, remember my tips on eating out, and away you go. Airline and steamship companies are most co-operative if notified ahead of your "special" diet. *Bon Voyage!* When you reach your destination and you don't want salt added to your food, be sure to say:

Arabic	*Ma Fii mil Hah*
Chinese	*wu yen*
English	*Without salt*
French	*sans sel*
German	*ohne Salz*
Greek	*horis alati*
Italian	*senza sale*
Japanese	*shio nuki*
Lithuanian	*be druskos*
Portuguese	*falto de sel*
Russian	*bez soli*
Spanish	*sin sal*
Swedish	*utan salt*
Yiddish	*una zaltz*

NOW DON'T EAT YOUR TOOTHPASTE . . . 15

for chemically pure precipitated calcium carbonate. What's

9 Now Don't Eat Your Toothpaste or Swallow the Ocean

I was so carried away with low-sodium and no salt that when we were to go to the seashore the image of the great expanse of sea and all the sodium in that rolling blue surf didn't induce beautiful, restful thoughts of sitting on the white sand with no worries—because my husband loved to swim. I called the doctor. (I wasn't about to have my husband's progress halted by all those millions of grams of sodium rushing at him.) I think the doctor thought I was carrying this whole thing too far. He assured me that the salt wouldn't go through Ted's eyes, nose, or skin and that all he need do was to keep his mouth shut. He did and even swam before breakfast.

Then there was a problem of another kind with water— a built-in softener on the cold-water spigot. Our doctor told us if we had one we had to take it out. We didn't, but I had always wanted one (heavens, everything seemed to have sodium). Someday, we will have one on the hot side. Then my bath will be bubbly, and there won't be such a huge ring to scrub after our three grandsons have their bath all at once.

Store toothpaste and powder are all right to use if you don't eat them and do wash your mouth out with water after scrubbing with up and down strokes. Never use mouthwashes unless you use water to rinse again. Our good dentist found a sodium-free powder for us which is the basis of all toothpastes. Make your own. Madison Avenue won't tell you how, but I will. Ask your druggist for chemically pure precipitated calcium carbonate. What a mouthful! Mix it with a little glycerine as you use it. Your teeth will gleam.

When unsalty has a headache, he must ask his doctor what to do to relieve the ache. Most pain relievers and sedatives are high-sodium. There is always the ice bag. So don't give up. Some "alkalizers," antibiotics, cough medicines, and sedatives might also be taboo. There again your doctor knows about these things.

Some store-bought laxatives are off the list too. Prune juice has only 2 mg. of sodium in a half cup. Drink it. Remember you hired your doctor to take care of you, so ask him whenever you have any question pertaining to unsalty's special diet problems. I'm not an M.D. Just the Manager of my unsalty's Diet.

P.S. Just discovered the "stickum" on postage stamps and envelopes has sodium, so, no licks.

10 Herbs, Seasonings, Flavors, and Blends

He causèth the grass to grow for the cattle,
and herb for the service of man:
that he may bring forth food out of the earth;
And wine that maketh glad the heart of man.

PSALMS 104: 14–15

Herbs *are* a special service to unsalty and salty—and it is exciting to be able to create a tasty dish without the use of salt. If you have never used herbs in cooking don't be concerned over amounts because these recipes show exact amounts. Later on you can do your own experimenting. You *will* have fun! It's like being talented enough to paint a beautiful picture.

Now you are ready to go shopping and spend the best money you have ever spent. Buy an herb rack if you feel rich. Then start buying like mad. I love the dear little bottles. But boxes or cans are fine, too, as is anything that contains herbs.

Here's What to Buy as a Start

HERBS AND SPICES

Allspice
Basil
Bay leaf
Caraway seed
Chervil
Chili con carne
   seasoning powder
Chives (dried)
Cinnamon
Cloves
Cumin
Curry
Dill (ground and seed)
Fennel
Garlic powder
Ginger
Mace
Marjoram
Mint (dried)

Mustard
Nutmeg
Onion powder
Oregano
Paprika
Parsley, dried
   (careful! 1 teaspoon has
   29 milligrams sodium)
Pepper, whole black
   (ask Santa for a pepper
   mill)
Poultry seasoning
   (read label)
Rosemary
Sage
Savory
Tarragon
Thyme

VINEGARS

Cider
Wine (a little higher in sodium)
White

WINE

1 bottle red
1 bottle white
1 bottle sherry (not cooking sherry)

You really didn't need the new hat, did you?

My parents might not have understood the use of wine in my recipes. Maybe they would if they had known that the alcoholic content is destroyed in the cooking and just the lovely flavor and aroma remain. Anyway, it won't raise unsalty's blood pressure if used in the prescribed amounts; but salt could, in any amount.

11 The Health or New-Vigor Store

Unsalty can't eat the black molasses (the kind they say makes you young in a hurry) sold in the health store, but the health store is, nevertheless, a good place to visit. New items are always arriving on the shelves. Last time there were low-sodium cornflakes, with no cut-out on the box or toy inside. I used the cornflakes in my meat loaf when there was not enough wheat germ, and the loaf was fine. Try it.

You must continue to read labels even in health stores. I bought a can of soup that said "No Salt Added," and later noticed that the sodium content was not listed. Always beware. I'll take the soup back when I buy some more low-sodium cheese. Most of the items are wonderful for unsalty.

Some Health Store Items and Their Sodium Contents

These are all dietetic low-sodium products.

	MILLIGRAMS SODIUM	CALORIES
1 beef bouillon cube	31.0	11
1 chicken bouillon cube	10.0	12

	MILLIGRAMS SODIUM	CALORIES
1 slice bread	4.0	75
(The bread we use has 2 mg. but 4 mg. is an average of 7 low-sodium types of bread.)		
1 tablespoon catsup	0.7	17
1 oz. low-sodium cheese	2.7	100
1 tablespoon chili sauce	0.7	17
1 tablespoon low-sodium cottage cheese	3.0	15
1 tablespoon mayonnaise	6.0	92
1 cup fresh low-sodium milk	12.0	166
1 quart low-sodium dry milk (reconstituted)	28.0	315
1 tablespoon mustard	1.5	16
1 tablespoon peanut butter	7.0	100
3 pickles (sliced)	1.0	4
½ cup salmon (canned)	31.0	85
½ cup stewed tomatoes	7.0	25
½ cup tomato juice	6.0	28
1 tablespoon tomato paste	4.0	14
½ cup tuna fish (canned)	31.0	122
1 teaspoon Worcestershire sauce	1.2	Unknown

For traveling long distances, you can buy low-sodium bread in cans. This bread is unsliced, and the 9 oz. can has 3.8 mg. of sodium.

12 When You Drink "Adam's Ale" Outside of Your Town

PUBLIC WATER SUPPLIES

MILLIGRAMS OF SODIUM IN 8 OUNCES (ONE CUPFUL)

Aberdeen, S.D.	48.0	Cheyenne, Wyo.	0.7
Albany, N.Y.	0.4	Chicago, Ill.	0.7
Albuquerque, N.M.	12.0	Cincinnati, Ohio	1.6
Annapolis, Md.	0.4	Cleveland, Ohio	2.3
Ann Arbor, Mich.	4.8	Columbia, S.C.	0.9
Atlanta, Ga.	0.4	Columbus, Ohio	12.0
Augusta, Me.	0.4	Concord, N.H.	0.4
Austin, Tex.	7.2	Crandall, Tex.	408.0
Baltimore, Md.	0.7	Dallas, Tex.	7.2
Baton Rouge, La.	21.6	Denver, Colo.	7.2
Beloit, Wis.	1.1	Des Moines, Iowa	2.3
Biloxi, Miss.	55.2	Detroit, Mich.	0.7
Birmingham, Ala.	4.8	Dover, Ill.	4.8
Bismarck, N.D.	14.4	Durham, N.C.	0.9
Boise, Ida.	4.8	El Paso, Tex.	16.8
Boston, Mass.	0.7	Evansville, Ind.	4.8
Brownsville, Tex.	14.4	Fargo, N.D.	12.0
Buffalo, N.Y.	1.6	Frankfort, Ky.	0.7
Burlington, Vt.	0.4	Galesburg, Ill.	72.0
Carson City, Nev.	0.9	Galveston, Tex.	81.6
Charleston, S.C.	2.3	Harrisburg, Pa.	0.4
Charleston, W.Va.	0.7	Hartford, Conn.	0.4
Charlotte, N.C.	0.7	Helena, Mont.	0.7
Charlottesville, Va.	0.4	Houston, Tex.	38.4

MILLIGRAMS OF SODIUM IN 8 OUNCES (ONE CUPFUL)

Huntington, W.Va.	7.2	Oklahoma City, Okla.	23.6
Indianapolis, Ind.	2.3	Olympia, Wash.	1.1
Iowa City, Iowa	1.1	Omaha, Nebr.	18.8
Jackson, Miss.	0.9	Philadelphia, Pa.	4.8
Jacksonville, Fla.	2.3	Phoenix, Ariz.	25.9
Jefferson City, Mo.	7.2	Pierre, S.D.	21.6
Jersey City, N.J.	0.7	Pittsburgh, Pa.	14.1
Kansas City, Kans.	9.4	Portland, Me.	0.4
Kansas City, Mo.	23.6	Portland, Ore.	0.2
Lansing, Mich.	2.3	Providence, R.I.	0.4
Lincoln, Nebr.	7.2	Raleigh, N.C.	0.9
Little Rock, Ark.	0.2	Reno, Nev.	1.1
Los Angeles, Calif.		Richmond, Va.	1.6
aqueduct source	14.1	Rochester, Minn.	1.6
metropolitan source	40.1	Rochester, N.Y.	0.7
river	12.0	Sacramento, Calif.	0.7
Louisville, Ky.	4.8	Santa Fe, N.M.	0.9
Madison, Wis.	0.9	St. Louis, Mo.	12.0
Manchester, N.H.	0.4	St. Paul, Minn.	1.1
Marion, Ohio	40.8	Salem, Ore.	0.4
Memphis, Tenn.	4.8	Salt Lake City, Utah	1.8
Miami, Fla.	4.8	San Diego, Calif.	12.0
Milwaukee, Wis.	0.7	San Francisco, Calif.	2.3
Minneapolis, Minn.	1.1	Seattle, Wash.	0.4
Minot, N.D.	60.0	Sioux Falls, S.D.	2.3
Montgomery, Ala.	1.8	Springfield, Ill.	1.8
Montpelier, Vt.	0.2	Syracuse, N.Y.	0.4
Nashville, Tenn.	0.7	Tallahassee, Fla.	0.7
Nevada, Mo.	77.8	Topeka, Kans.	2.3
Newark, N.J.	0.4	Trenton, N.J.	0.2
New Haven, Conn.	0.7	Tucson, Ariz.	7.2
New Orleans, La.	2.3	Washington, D.C.	0.7
New York, N.Y.	0.7	Wichita, Kans.	12.0
Oakland, Calif.	0.7	Wilmington, Del.	1.8

If your town or city isn't on this list, call your local Board of Health, which will be happy to inform you of the sodium content of your water supply.

These recipes have not included the sodium content of the water used in the preparation of the foods. If you are on a very strict low-sodium diet your doctor may wish you to count the milligrams of sodium in your local water supply.

One winter the salt used on the streets during the winter storms ran into our local public-water supply. This is a serious situation for unsalty. Register with your local Board of Health, and if the sodium content of the water reaches a dangerous level because of this condition you will be notified and fresh water will be sent to you.

13   Low-Sodium in Basic Nutrition

MILK GROUP

Leading source of calcium, high-quality protein, riboflavin, and Vitamin A needed for bones and teeth.

Adults—2 or more cups a day

High in sodium, so your doctor must set the amount. Low-sodium fresh milk or dry milk should be substituted if your doctor says so. Low-sodium cheese is included in this group.

MEAT GROUP

Valued for their protein, iron, thiamine, riboflavin, and niacin. Needed for growth and repair of body tissues. High in sodium so your doctor must set the amount.

2 servings a day

Beef
Ham (only canned low-sodium)
Lamb
Liver
Pork
Veal
Poultry

Fish (remember—only fresh fish or canned low-
    sodium)
Eggs

'ALTERNATES

All these are low-sodium touchables

Dry beans
Dry peas
Lentils
Unsalted nuts
Low-sodium peanut butter

VEGETABLE FRUIT GROUP

Important for vitamins and minerals. Most are touchable. Vitamin A needed for growth, vision, skin. See
Vegetable Touchable list. Vitamin C for gums and body
tissues.

4 or more servings a day

1 citrus fruit or other fruit or vegetable high in
    Vitamin C
1 dark green vegetable for Vitamin A
Other vegetables and fruits, including potatoes

BREAD CEREAL GROUP

Important amounts of protein, iron, B Vitamins. Supplies energy.

4 servings

Low-sodium bread. See List of Bread Touchables.

FAT AND OIL GROUP

Growth and resistance to disease, produces heat.
  Unsalted butter or margarine
  Vegetable oil

Untouchables and Touchables

I found myself in the deepest dilemma in checking sodium
and caloric counts. The sodium tables varied as did the
caloric counts. This, of course, has an explanation. Water,
climate, and soil conditions are among the many factors
that affect the analysis. There is no standard reference for
the exact sodium and caloric content of each food. One
could argue the figures indefinitely. I'm sure vegetables
from around Kansas City are of a different sodium level
from those in Millburn, New Jersey. Wherever reasonable
the highest calculation of an assayer was used in these
tables.

14   Untouchables

Copy this page and place carefully in your wallet or purse.
To you it is more valuable than money.

When food is transported between states, federal law requires the label on all packaged and canned foods to show whether food contains salt in any form.

DON'T BUY FOOD CONTAINING:

Salt (sodium chloride)	To season, to can, and to process food
Baking soda (sodium bicarbonate)	To leaven bread and cakes
	To "alkalize" for indigestion
Brine (salt and water)	To check bacteria growth
	To clean and blanch vegetables and fruits
	To flavor food
	To freeze and to can certain foods
Monosodium glutamate	To flavor food
Baking powder	To leaven breads and cakes

Di-Sodium phosphate	Found in some quick-cooking cereals and processed cheeses
Sodium alginate	To smooth texture of chocolate milk and ice cream
Sodium benzoate	To preserve condiments
Sodium hydroxide	To soften and loosen skin of certain fruits and vegetables as olives
Sodium propionate	To inhibit growth of mold in pasteurized cheese and in some breads and cakes
Sodium sulfite	To bleach fruits, to obtain artificial color as in maraschino cherries, glazed fruit To preserve certain dried fruit
Na	Chemist's symbol for sodium

UNTOUCHABLE SEASONINGS, FLAVORS AND BLENDS

Bouillon cube
(except low-sodium)
Candies
(commercial and
homemade with salt)
Catsup
(except low-sodium)
Celery flakes

Celery salt
Chili sauce
(except low-sodium)
Cocoa
(instant mixes)
French dressing
(except low-sodium)
Garlic salt

Gelatin, flavored
Horseradish with salt
Mayonnaise
  (except low-sodium)
Meat extracts
Meat sauces
  (salted)
Meat tenderizers
  (except low-sodium)
Molasses
Monosodium glutamate
Mustard
  (except low-sodium)
Olives
Onion salt
Pickles
  (except low-sodium)

Pudding mixes
  (except low-sodium)
Relishes
  (except low-sodium)
Rennet tablets
Salt
  (except what your
  doctor may allow you)
Salted nuts
Salt substitutes
  (except what your
  doctor allows)
Soy sauce
Sugar substitute
  (cyclamate sodium)
Worcestershire sauce
  (except low-sodium)

UNTOUCHABLE DRINKABLES

Carbonated beverages vary in sodium content. There are a few listed in the Touchable list with sodium content.

Cocoa instant mixes
Chocolate milk
Malted milk
Milk shakes
Salted buttermilk

UNTOUCHABLE VEGETABLES

All canned vegetables
  (except low-sodium)
All canned vegetable soups
  (except low-sodium)
Frozen peas and Lima
  beans
Artichokes

Beet greens
Beets
Celery
Dandelion greens
Kale
Mustard greens
Sauerkraut

Spinach
Swiss chard
White turnips

Some lists forbid
    carrots

UNTOUCHABLE MEATS

Bacon
Bologna
Brains
Chipped beef
Corned beef
Frankfurters
Ham
    (except canned
    low-sodium)
All canned meat soups
    and stews (except
    low-sodium)
Kidneys

Kosher meats [1]
Salt pork
Sausage
Smoked tongue
Liverwurst
Salami
Canned meat
    (except low-sodium)
Pickled meat
Salted meat
Smoked meat
Spiced meat

More Untouchables

Don't buy or eat:

BREADS AND THEIR FAMILIES

Commercial or homemade with salt

Bread
Crackers
Rolls
Cakes and cake mixes (except low-sodium)
Cookies
Waffles

---

[1] Kosher meat is salted. If you are on a low-sodium diet, Jewish law excuses from the consumption of Kosher meat.

Self-rising corn meal and flour

Quick-cooking cereals except Ralston, Maltex, and Wheatena

Dry cereals except puffed rice, puffed wheat, and shredded wheat

Salted popcorn, salted potato chips and pretzels

DAIRY AND FARM UNTOUCHABLES

All salted cheeses
Commercial and homemade
   salted ice cream and sherbet
Salted butter
Salted buttermilk

FISH UNTOUCHABLES

No frozen fish fillets	Clams
All canned fish	Cod, dried
(except low-sodium)	Cod, salted
All salted fish	Crabs
All shellfish	Herring
(except oysters[2])	Lobster
All smoked fish	Sardines
Anchovies	Scallops
Caviar	Shrimp

---

[2] If Doctor permits.

15   Touchables

In the cooking of meat, poultry, or fish, the shrinkage is approximately 25 per cent. For instance, 4 ounces of raw meat, poultry, or fish becomes 3 ounces cooked. However, the sodium content *doesn't* shrink and is valued in the raw weight.

All sodium contents of meats are figured after the removal of excess fat.

MEAT AND POULTRY TOUCHABLES

TOUCHABLES COOKED WEIGHT	MILLIGRAMS SODIUM	CALORIES
3 oz. beef	80	250
3 oz. chicken (white)	89	186
3 oz. duck breast	80	200
3 oz. pork	64	280
3 oz. rabbit	53	140
3 oz. turkey (white)	48	219

CAREFUL TOUCHABLES COOKED WEIGHT	MILLIGRAMS SODIUM	CALORIES
3 oz. chicken (dark)	124	196
3 oz. duck leg	108	228
3 oz. lamb	100	220
3 oz. liver (calf)	125	180
3 oz. sweetbreads	100	188
3 oz. tongue	90	220
3 oz. turkey (dark)	104	245
3 oz. veal	110	228

Unsalted gravy (if your doctor allows gravy) may be used from the portion of meat, fish, or chicken allowed in your diet. Divide the quantity of liquid left in the kettle by the number of servings to find the correct amount.

FRESH FISH TOUCHABLES

TOUCHABLES COOKED WEIGHT	MILLIGRAMS SODIUM	CALORIES
3 oz. bass	75	150
3 oz. bluefish	75	144
3 oz. cod	88	80
3 oz. flounder	64	75
3 oz. haddock	68	88
3 oz. halibut	60	144
3 oz. mackerel	60	204
3 oz. trout	60	116
9 medium oysters	90	280
3 oz. salmon	90	225
3 oz. sole	100	115
3 oz. swordfish	90	140
3 oz. tuna	90	225

I have an old-fashioned kitchen scale beside the stove. Besides being attractive, it is most useful. There is never a question about 3 ounces of cooked meat, poultry, or fish.

TOUCHABLE FRESH VEGETABLES

Frozen vegetables are permissible if processed without salt. Read label.

	MILLIGRAMS SODIUM	CALORIES
6 stalks asparagus	2.0	22
½ cup beans (green and wax)	1.0	23
½ cup beans (Lima)	1.0	100
½ cup broccoli	10.1	22
9 Brussels sprouts	11.0	60
1 cup cabbage (shredded)	12.8	20
1 large carrot[1]	48.0	20
½ cup cauliflower	18.0	15
1 ear sweet corn	3.0	85
1 cucumber	7.2	20
½ eggplant	8.4	48
4 escarole leaves	3.0	3
4 endive leaves	3.6	7
¼ head lettuce (solid)	12.0	13
8 large mushrooms	10.0	25
10 pods okra	1.0	30
1 medium onion	6.0	25
2 tablespoons parsley	2.0	2
½ cup peas	0.7	56
1 green pepper	1.0	16
1 potato (white)	4.0	97
1 potato (sweet)	12.0	183

[1] The assayers vary greatly on the sodium content of carrots. There are approximately 4 ounces in one large carrot, and one assayer determines the sodium content to be only 8.8 an ounce.

	MILLIGRAMS SODIUM	CALORIES
1 cup pumpkin	2.0	66
1 radish	3.0	2
½ cup summer squash	0.6	15
½ cup winter squash	0.6	45
1 tomato	3.0	30
½ cup turnip greens (cooked)	10.0	22
½ cup yellow turnips (cooked)	5.0	25
½ cup watercress	11.0	2

TOUCHABLE FRESH FRUITS

	MILLIGRAMS SODIUM	CALORIES
1 apple (skinned)	2.0	75
1 apricot	0.4	18
1 avocado	6.0	485
1 banana	1.4	99
½ cup blackberries	2.0	41
½ cup blueberries	1.0	43
¼ cantaloupe	6.0	18
½ cup cherries	3.0	40
1 cup coconut (grated)	18.4	352
1 cup cranberries	1.0	54
½ cup currants	1.3	30
½ grapefruit	3.0	75
30 grapes	3.5	70
½ cup lemon juice and pulp	2.0	32
1 mango	4.0	133
1 orange	2.0	70
1 papaya	6.0	43
1 peach	2.0	51
1 pear	2.0	60
½ cup pineapple	1.0	32
1 plum	0.6	29

	MILLIGRAMS SODIUM	CALORIES
1 cup raspberries	1.0	84
1 cup rhubarb	2.0	20
10 strawberries	0.8	35
1 tangerine	0.6	35
8 oz. watermelon	0.6	75

DAIRY AND FARM TOUCHABLES

	MILLIGRAMS SODIUM	CALORIES
1 tablespoon sweet or unsalted butter	0.7	100
8 oz. non-fat unsalted buttermilk	120.0	85
8 oz. evaporated milk (reconstituted)	126.0	166
8 oz. skim milk	127.9	87
8 oz. whole milk	122.0	166
8 oz. low-sodium dry milk (reconstituted)	7.0	79
8 oz. low-sodium fresh milk	12.0	166
8 oz. plain yogurt	117.0	120
8 oz. fruit yogurt	88.0	220
1 oz. low-sodium cheese	2.7	100
1 tablespoon low-sodium cottage cheese	3.0	15
1 tablespoon cream	5.7	49
1 tablespoon sour cream	5.7	49
1 tablespoon milk	7.6	11
1 egg	68.0	77
1 egg yolk	13.0	61
1 egg white	55.0	16

BREAD TOUCHABLES AND THEIR FAMILIES

	MILLIGRAMS SODIUM	CALORIES
BREAD		
1 slice low-sodium bread	4.0	75
1 low-sodium roll	4.0	75
1 low-sodium melba toast	1.6	15
1 matzoh (Passover)	0.2	112
CEREALS		
½ cup barley (uncooked)	3.0	400
1 cup low-sodium cornflakes	2.0	165
½ cup corn meal (cooked)	0.5	60
½ cup popped corn	0.4	60
½ cup cream of wheat (cooked)	1.0	60
½ cup farina (cooked)	4.0	68
½ cup macaroni (cooked)	1.0	114
½ cup Maltex (cooked)	2.0	71
½ cup rolled oats (cooked)	0.4	77
½ cup Ralston (cooked)	0.4	71
1 cup puffed rice	0.5	54
½ cup white rice (uncooked)	2.0	344
½ cup spaghetti (cooked)	1.5	96
2 tablespoons tapioca	1.0	68
½ cup Wheatena (cooked)	0.4	77
1 tablespoon wheat germ	0.1	28
1 cup puffed wheat	1.0	50
1 biscuit shredded wheat	4.0	103
FAMILIES		
1 tablespoon cornstarch	0.5	29
1 cup flour	2.7	400
1 tablespoon flour	0.1	25
1 teaspoon cream of tartar	8.0	Negligible
1 tablespoon yeast (compressed)	0.6	20

	MILLIGRAMS SODIUM	CALORIES

OTHER FAMILIES

	MILLIGRAMS SODIUM	CALORIES
1 tablespoon unflavored gelatin	3.6	34
1 tablespoon vinegar (cider and distilled)	Negligible	2
1 tablespoon red wine vinegar	4.0	2
1 tablespoon white wine vinegar	5.0	2

OIL TOUCHABLES

	MILLIGRAMS SODIUM	CALORIES
1 tablespoon low-sodium margarine	1.5	100
1 tablespoon low-sodium mayonnaise	6.0	92
½ cup corn oil	0.3	1000
½ cup olive oil	0.3	1000
1 tablespoon olive oil	Negligible	125
½ cup safflower oil	0.3	1000
½ cup soy bean oil	0.3	1000
½ cup vegetable shortening	0.8	880

TOUCHABLE SWEETS

	MILLIGRAMS SODIUM	CALORIES
1 tablespoon honey	1.5	62
1 tablespoon jam or jelly without added preservatives	1.0	55
1 cup white sugar	0.8	770

	MILLIGRAMS SODIUM	CALORIES
1 tablespoon white sugar	Negligible	48
1 tablespoon powdered sugar	0.1	31
1 tablespoon brown sugar	3.4	51
1 tablespoon maple syrup (pure)	2.8	57
1 square unsweetened chocolate	3.0	142
1 marshmallow	3.1	20

Fine low-sodium candies may be bought in some shops specializing in candies. You must check to find out what sweetener is used. If you like gum, one stick has 1 mg. sodium (not the kind that is covered with candy).

DRINKABLE TOUCHABLES

	MILLIGRAMS SODIUM	CALORIES
1 teaspoon cocoa	2.0	7
1 teaspoon coffee (instant)	1.7	0
1 tablespoon coffee (regular)	1.5	0
1 teaspoon Postum (instant)	0.4	2
1 teaspoon Sanka	0.1	0
1 teaspoon tea	0.1	0

FRUIT JUICES

½ cup apple cider	1.0	62
½ cup apple juice	6.0	62
½ cup apricot juice	4.0	51
½ cup cranberry juice	3.0	90
½ cup grapefruit juice	2.0	65
½ cup grape juice	4.0	85
½ cup lemon juice	2.0	32

	MILLIGRAMS SODIUM	CALORIES
½ cup orange juice	2.5	54
½ cup pineapple juice	0.6	60
½ cup prune juice	2.0	85
½ cup tangerine juice	2.0	47
½ cup fresh tomato juice	6.0	25
½ cup canned low-sodium tomato juice	6.0	28

DRINKABLE BEVERAGES

6½ oz. Coca Cola	1.8	80
8 oz. ginger ale	18.4	75
7 oz. Seven-up	13.9	66
8 oz. White Rock club soda	1.7	80

DRINKABLE MILKS

1 cup whole milk	122.0	166
1 cup skim milk	127.9	87
1 cup low-sodium dry milk (liquified)	7.0	79
1 cup low-sodium fresh milk	12.0	166

DRINKABLE WITH DOCTOR'S PERMISSION

12 oz. beer	4.0–17.0	170
1 oz. brandy	1.3	80
1 oz. gin	0.2	70
1 oz. rum	0.5	90
1 oz. whiskey	0.9	86
8 oz. red table wine	16.0	168
8 oz. dry sauterne	22.0	168
1 tablespoon sherry	2.3	22

NUT TOUCHABLES

	MILLIGRAMS SODIUM	CALORIES
20 almonds	5.0	170
4 brazil	4.0	125
8 cashews	4.0	171
6 chestnuts	1.0	49
20 hazelnuts	1.0	200
30 peanuts	3.2	171
6 pecans (whole)	2.4	185
6 walnuts	2.0	156

TOUCHABLE DRIED VEGETABLES

	MILLIGRAMS SODIUM	CALORIES
½ cup split peas	25.0	354
½ cup lentils	4.0	347
½ cup soybeans	4.0	348
½ cup navy beans	1.0	321
½ cup kidney beans	2.8	400
½ cup pea beans	1.0	321

CANNED FRUIT TOUCHABLES

Most canned fruit may be used (read label). Here are a few with sodium milligram and caloric content.

	MILLIGRAMS SODIUM	CALORIES
½ cup applesauce	3.6	92
½ cup apricots	5.0	90

	MILLIGRAMS SODIUM	CALORIES
½ cup cherries	1.0	61
½ cup cranberry sauce	1.2	274
½ cup grapefruit	3.0	100
2 halves peaches	3.0	79
2 halves pears	2.0	79
2 slices pineapple, small	1.0	100
3 plums	3.0	100

TOUCHABLE DRIED FRUIT

Sometimes SODIUM SULFITE has been added to dried fruit. Read label.

	MILLIGRAMS SODIUM	CALORIES
5 apricots	5.0	82
2 dates	Negligible	43
3 peaches	5.0	133
8 prunes	3.0	144
1 tablespoon raisins	3.0	35
2 figs (large)	16.0	114

TOUCHABLE SEASONINGS, FLAVORS, AND BLENDS

See, this list is longer than the untouchables.

The sodium content of the following is low and because they are used in small amounts you may use them as you wish.

HERBS AND SPICES

Allspice
Anise seed
Basil
Bay leaf
Caraway seed
Cardamom
Celery seed (ground or whole)[2]
Chevril
Chili con carne seasoning powder[3]
Chives
Cinnamon
Cloves (ground or whole)
Coriander (ground or whole)
Cumin
Curry
Dill (ground and seed)
Fennel
Garlic bud
Garlic powder and chips
Ginger (ground or whole)
Horseradish
Juniper

Lemon peel
Mace (ground or whole)
Marjoram
Mint
Mushrooms, powdered
Mustard, dry
Nutmeg
Onion, instant
Orange peel
Oregano
Paprika
Parsley, dried[4]
Pepper, black, red and white
Poppy seed
Poultry seasoning
Pumpkin pie spice
Rosemary
Saffron
Sage
Savory
Sesame seeds
Tarragon
Thyme
Turmeric

FLAVORS

Almond extract
Cocoa
Lemon juice

Lemon extract
Onion, fresh, juice or sliced

[2] Never celery flakes or celery salt. Celery seed has only 2 mg. of sodium in 1 teaspoon. Celery flakes have 115 mg. of sodium in 1 teaspoon and celery salt has 840 mg. of sodium in 1 teaspoon!

[3] Chili con carne seasoning powder has 1 mg. of sodium in 1 teaspoon. Chili powder has 57 mg. of sodium in 1 teaspoon.

[4] Dried parsley has 29 mg. of sodium in 1 teaspoon. Fresh parsley has 1 mg. of sodium in 1 tablespoon.

Orange extract

Green or red pepper

Peppermint extract

Pimento

Saccharin (if doctor says so)

Salt substitutes (if doctor says so)

Sugar

Vanilla extract, without salt

Vinegar, white, cider or wine

Wine (if doctor says so)

Walnut extract

BLENDS

All low-sodium dietetic:

Bouillon cubes

Catsup

Chili sauce

Mustard

Pickles

Tomato sauce

Worcestershire sauce

16   Enlightenment by Contrast

It is true that we learn by comparison. To understand why certain foods are forbidden to unsalty, I have called these lists "Enlightenment by Contrast." Compare the sodium content on these lists with the same foods on the Touchable lists. Now do you see what salt does to the sodium content of foods when added during the processing? The fresh vegetables listed below are omitted from your list only because they contain a high natural sodium content and the reason they are taboo is very simple. Your doctor wants you to keep the protein and calcium in your diet at a proper level. As you know, our best supplies of protein and calcium come from animal sources, and they are high in sodium. It would not be good sense to eat a half cup of Swiss chard and use 100 milligrams of sodium of your daily count when you can have a half cup of string beans and use only 2 milligrams of sodium. The other 98 milligrams you can save and use toward your milk and meat allowance for that day.

Thank goodness for men and women who devote their lives to research in the fields of medicine and nutrition.

FRESH VEGETABLES	MILLIGRAMS SODIUM	CALORIES
1 large artichoke	41.3	50
½ cup beets	40.8	35
½ cup beet greens, cooked	148.4	33
2 stalks celery	58.3	2
½ cup Swiss chard, cooked	100.0	15
½ cup dandelion greens, cooked	86.8	52
½ cup kale, cooked	40.0	23
½ cup mustard greens, cooked	42.0	16
½ cup spinach, cooked	75.0	25
½ cup white turnip	26.0	20

FROZEN VEGETABLES	MILLIGRAMS SODIUM	CALORIES
½ cup Lima beans	356.0	90
½ cup peas	308.0	70

CANNED VEGETABLES	MILLIGRAMS SODIUM	CALORIES
6 stalks asparagus	394.0	22
½ cup green beans	258.0	20
½ cup Lima beans	248.0	95
½ cup mushrooms	536.8	15
½ cup spinach	290.0	23
½ cup beets	40.8	35
½ cup carrots	204.0	20
½ cup peas	220.0	73
½ cup tomato juice	262.8	26
½ cup tomatoes	25.0	23
½ cup corn	170.0	70

MORE ENLIGHTENMENT BY CONTRAST

	MILLIGRAMS SODIUM	CALORIES
1 slice salted bread	140.0	75
1 tablespoon salted butter	150.0	100
1 tablespoon salted margarine	166.0	100
½ cup ice cream	75.0	147
1 tablespoon malted milk, dry	36.0	37
1 tablespoon condensed milk, sweetened	26.0	64
1 candy bar, average	85.0	260
1 package gelatin (fruit)	281.0	324

CONTRAST

Look at the difference!

	MILLIGRAMS SODIUM
1 tablespoon low-sodium catsup	0.7
1 tablespoon catsup	*221.0*
1 ounce lean beef	20.0
1 ounce dried beef	*1219.0*
1 low-sodium bouillon cube beef	31.0
1 bouillon cube	*960.0*
½ cup cabbage	12.8
½ cup sauerkraut	*536.0*
1 ounce low-sodium cheddar cheese	2.7
1 ounce cheddar cheese	*198.0*
1 cucumber	14.4
1 dill pickle	*1900.0*

	MILLIGRAMS SODIUM
1 ounce fresh codfish	22.0
1 ounce salted codfish	*2296.0*
1 ounce low-sodium ham	14.0
1 ounce cured ham	*312.0*
8 unsalted peanuts	0.5
8 salted peanuts	*35.0*
1 tablespoon low-sodium peanut butter	7.0
1 tablespoon peanut butter	*19.0*
10 unsalted potato chips	1.0
10 salted potato chips	*70.0*
½ cup unsalted popcorn	0.2
½ cup salted popcorn	*160.0*
1 teaspoon low-sodium prepared mustard	1.5
1 teaspoon prepared mustard	*66.0*
1 tablespoon low-sodium Worcestershire sauce	3.6
1 tablespoon Worcestershire sauce	*315.0*

Isn't this a revelation?

17 Quid Pro Quo (Equivalents)

3 teaspoons=1 tablespoon
1 fluid ounce=2 tablespoons
¼ cup=4 tablespoons
⅓ cup=5 tablespoons plus 1 teaspoon
1 cup=½ pint
2 cups=1 pint
4 cups=1 quart
¼ pound butter=½ cup
1 medium lemon=3 tablespoons juice
1 medium orange=6 to 8 tablespoons juice
1 grated orange rind=1 tablespoon
30 c.c.=1 ounce

ABBREVIATIONS
oz.   ounce
mg.   milligrams
c.c.   cubic centimeter

18 Breakfast, Bread, and Because

If you want to make your own bread, go ahead. I don't want to. Low-sodium bread can be bought most everywhere. My wonderful butcher, Joe, buys the bread in quantities and stores it in his freezer. Wish I had a new refrigerator with a large freezer. It would be valuable because, as you know by now, low-sodium bread, butter, and margarine are happier in a freezer. Only one more payment to Smith College, then I'll buy one. College is more important than a new freezer as long as one has a Joe.

Get your bread board out.

3 *tablespoons sugar*
3 *tablespoons vegetable shortening*
1 *cup lukewarm water*
½ *cake compressed yeast*

3 *cups plus 1 tablespoon flour*
1 *tablespoon unsalted butter or margarine*

Put the sugar, shortening in a large bowl. Add the water. Sprinkle the yeast over the lukewarm mixture. Mix. Add half of the flour and stir with wooden spoon. Add rest of flour and stir in a lot. Knead the dough with floured hands until smooth and place in greased bowl. Spread melted butter or margarine over dough, cover with towel and let rise in warm place until dough doubles in size. Knead again. Shape into loaf. Place in greased loaf pan. Spread rest of butter or margarine on top, cover. Let rise until double in bulk. Bake at 400 degrees for about 30 to 35 minutes. Dough will rise twice as fast without salt.

BAKING POWDER

If you want to bake and bake and make your favorite cakes, cookies, and breads, you can buy sodium-free baking powder in health stores or on the dietetic shelves of some supermarkets. If not, have your druggist make it up for you:

Cornstarch	28.0 grams
Potassium bicarbonate	39.8 grams
Potassium bi-tartare	56.1 grams
Tartaric acid	7.5 grams

Good Morning

Hot cereals cooked without salt are fine with a topping of warm fruit and honey and a sprinkle of nutmeg.

POACHED EGG

We call this a French egg.

1 egg
2 teaspoons vinegar
1 slice low-sodium bread
1 teaspoon unsalted
butter or margarine

Pepper to taste
If you like—a sprinkle of
curry, sage, or mustard

Fill saucepan ⅔ full of water. Bring water to boil. Add vinegar. Stir water fast until a whirlpool has formed; break egg in middle. Cook 1½ to 2 minutes. Remove with slotted spoon. Place on toasted bread. Top with unsalted butter or margarine and seasonings.

Total recipe, 72 mg. sodium and 187 calories.

If for tomorrow's breakfast you would like a scrambled egg, try flavoring the egg with savory and basil or dill.

EGGS BENEDICT A LA UNSALTY

Poach egg any saltless way you wish. Place poached egg in individual flat dish. Place on top 2 teaspoons of warmed low-sodium mayonnaise which has been mixed with ½ teaspoon lemon juice. Dash of sage, curry, or mustard if you like. Try turmeric, it's good.

Total per individual dish, 72 mg. sodium and 139 calories.

UNSALTY'S FRENCH TOAST

3 *slices low-sodium bread*　　¼ *cup sugar*
1 *egg, beaten*　　　　　　　½ *cup sifted all-purpose*
⅛ *cup milk*　　　　　　　　Nutmeg

Mix egg, milk, sugar, and vanilla. Remove crust and soak bread in egg mixture for 5 minutes. Brown on greased griddle. Sprinkle with nutmeg. Serve with honey, jelly, or pure maple syrup.

Per slice, 32 mg. sodium and 174 calories.

French toast also can be cooked in the oven. Dip each slice in mixture. Place slices on oiled baking dish. Bake in 450-degree oven for 7 minutes on one side, then turn and brown 5 minutes longer. If you use grape jelly, add a sprinkle of cardamom.

BREAKFAST, BREAD, AND BECAUSE 53

UNSALTY'S PANCAKES

Really French crêpes and delicious. You may use your favorite pancake recipe, but substitute low-sodium baking powder and omit the salt.

½ cup sifted all-purpose flour
1 egg
1 egg yolk
5 tablespoons milk (about)

3 tablespoons currant or red raspberry jelly
Powdered sugar
⅛ teaspoon mace

Combine flour, egg, egg yolk, and milk. Beat with rotary beater until smooth. Cover, chill ½ hour in refrigerator—or make night before. Heat heavy small iron skillet, wipe out with paper which has been dipped in unsalted butter or margarine. Pour in enough batter to barely cover bottom of skillet. Brown pancakes on both sides. Remove from skillet, spread with unsalted margarine or butter and serve. If you like, roll up jelly-roll fashion and sprinkle with a little powdered sugar. Place under broiler to glaze. Serve with pure maple syrup or honey.

YIELD 12 PANCAKES. *Per pancake, 11 mg. sodium and 48 calories.*

CRANBERRY AND BANANA TOAST

1 slice low-sodium bread
1 teaspoon unsalted butter or margarine
1 tablespoon cranberry sauce

½ banana, sliced
1 teaspoon brown sugar
¼ teaspoon cinnamon or allspice

Place bread under broiler and toast on one side, spread

butter or margarine on other side, spread with cranberry sauce, cover with sliced banana, sprinkle with brown sugar and cinnamon or allspice. Broil slowly until bananas are light brown and the sauce bubbling. Try a sprinkle of anise sometimes.

Per serving, 7 mg. sodium and 211 calories.

APPLESAUCE TOAST

1 *tablespoon unsalted butter or margarine*	*Cinnamon and nutmeg to taste*
1½ *tablespoons sugar*	*Low-sodium bread*
1 *cup applesauce*	

Melt butter or margarine, add sugar, applesauce, cinnamon, and nutmeg, spread on bread, and toast in oven.

Total for sauce, 9 mg. sodium and 356 calories. Per tablespoon, negligible sodium and 21 calories.

SPOON BREAD

This is for Southern unsalties. Spoon bread is a part of their blood and they shall have it.

1 *cup corn meal*	1½ *cups milk, scalded*
1 *cup water*	1 *egg, well beaten*
½ *cup unsalted butter or margarine*	

Combine corn meal and water. Cook over low heat, stirring occasionally, for 15 minutes. Remove from heat. Melt butter or margarine in scalded milk, add to corn mixture and mix until smooth. Slowly stir beaten egg into hot mixture. Pour into oiled 1-quart casserole. Bake at 350 degrees for 35 minutes. Serve with pure maple syrup.

10 SERVINGS. *Per serving, 27 mg. sodium and 139 calories. 1 tablespoon syrup, 3 mg. sodium and 57 calories.*

JOHNNYCAKES

Winter and autumn days and a cozy fire go well with johnnycakes. Try baked bananas, Astoria Salad* (apple and walnut) with them for Sunday supper.

1 *cup white corn meal*	1¼ *cups boiling water*
1 *teaspoon sugar*	¼ *cup milk*
⅛ *teaspoon mace*	

Warm utensils. Mix corn meal with sugar and mace. Pour boiling water over dry ingredients and mix well. When thoroughly mixed add milk. Drop by tablespoons on hot heavy skillet. Turn and cook on other side as you do pancakes. Serve with unsalted butter or margarine and jelly or honey.

YIELD 12 CAKES. *Per cake, 3 mg. sodium and 38 calories.*

Sandwiches

So many fine sandwiches can be made for unsalty. Leftover chicken, meat, even fish can be sliced or ground and mixed with low-sodium mayonnaise or herb butter. For herb butter try mixing unsalted butter or margarine with herbs, lemon juice, chives, dill, onion or garlic powder, mustard, or even a little wine. Try combinations that taste interesting to you.

SANDWICH SEASONINGS

CHICKEN-TURKEY

Cranberry sauce
Curry
Mustard—dry or low-
   sodium prepared

Pineapple bits
Sage
Thyme

FISH

Curry
Dill
Garlic powder
Lemon juice
Mustard—dry or low-
   sodium prepared

Onion powder
Sage
Turmeric

MEAT

BEEF

Allspice
Dill
Mustard—dry or low-
   sodium prepared
Nutmeg

Onion powder
Oregano
Thyme
Worcestershire sauce—
   low-sodium

LAMB

Curry
Dill
Garlic powder
Mint

Mint jelly—pure
Onion powder
Rosemary

PORK
    Chopped apples   Garlic powder
    Applesauce   Onion powder
    Dill   Sage

VEAL
    Curry   Marjoram
    Ginger   Oregano

APPLE SANDWICH

This is a treat, and is not like the apple of discord that started the Trojan War. Remember? Paris gave the apple to Aphrodite who promised him the fairest of women, Helen of Troy.

Wash apple, core, and cut crosswise into ¼-inch slices. Spread half the slices with peanut butter and top with the other apple slices.

1 apple, 2 mg. sodium and 75 calories.

1 tablespoon low-sodium peanut butter, 7 mg. sodium and 100 calories.

TOASTED CHEESE WITH TOMATO SANDWICH

Spread low-sodium bread with unsalted butter or margarine. Add sliced low-sodium cheese, and top with sliced tomato. Sprinkle with dry mustard and basil. Broil until cheese is bubbly.

1 tablespoon unsalted margarine, 1.5 mg. sodium and 100 calories.

1 ounce low-sodium cheese, 2.7 mg. sodium and 100 calories.

1 tomato, 3 mg. sodium and 30 calories.

EGG SALAD SANDWICH

If unsalty has not had his egg for breakfast and the doctor allows an egg a day, try this. Remember one egg has 68 mg. of sodium, and that is a lot. Most of the sodium is in the white—the yolk has only 13 mg. of sodium. Combine chopped egg and ½ tablespoon of low-sodium mayonnaise (3 mg.), a dash or two of herb vinegar and black pepper, and ½ tablespoon of chopped chives or parsley. Spread between unsalty's bread.

1 egg, 68 mg. sodium and 77 calories.
½ tablespoon low-sodium mayonnaise, 3 mg. sodium and 46 calories.

FIG SANDWICH

1 *cup figs*   1 *teaspoon lemon juice*
½ *cup hot water*   3 *chopped walnuts*

Chop figs fine. Cook to a paste with water. Add lemon juice. Cool. Spread on low-sodium bread and dust with ground nuts.

2 figs, 16 mg. sodium and 114 calories.
3 chopped walnuts, 1 mg. sodium and 78 calories.

HONEY-BUTTER SANDWICH

We think it might have been cheaper for us to have invested in our own beehive. Honey is a wonderful food for the unsalty without too much of a weight problem. There are 62 calories in a tablespoon, but only 1.5 mg. of sodium.

Combine equal parts of honey and unsalted butter or

margarine. Spread between unsalty's bread. Toast bread. It's better.

1 tablespoon honey, 1.5 mg. sodium and 62 calories.
1 tablespoon unsalted margarine, 1.5 mg. sodium and 100 calories.

MUSHROOM SANDWICH OR CANAPE SPREAD

I just counted the mushrooms in ¾ of a pound. There were 12 of the large ones.

¾ lb. mushrooms	¼ teaspoon pepper
¼ cup unsalted butter or margarine	2 teaspoons chopped fresh parsley
½ tablespoon cornstarch	

Chop mushrooms fine. Sauté in butter or margarine. Remove 1 tablespoon butter, cool. Lightly blend butter with cornstarch in separate pan. Stir until smooth. Add to mushrooms. Add pepper and cook, stirring until thick and smooth. Mix in parsley. Chill.

Total recipe, 21 mg. sodium and 450 calories.

PEANUT BUTTER AND RAISIN SANDWICH

1 tablespoon low-sodium peanut butter, 7 mg. sodium and 100 calories.
1 tablespoon raisins, 3 mg. sodium and 35 `calories.

Mix and spread on low-sodium bread.

PEANUT BUTTER AND CUCUMBER PICKLE SANDWICH

*1 tablespoon low-sodium peanut butter, 7 mg. sodium
and 100 calories.*
*3 slices low-sodium cucumber pickles, chopped, 1 mg.
sodium and 4 calories.*
1 teaspoon minced onion, 0.3 mg. sodium and 1 calorie.

Mix and spread on low-sodium bread.

PEANUT BUTTER AND HONEY SANDWICH

*1 tablespoon low-sodium peanut butter, 7 mg. sodium
and 100 calories.*
1 tablespoon honey, 2 mg. sodium and 62 calories.

Mix and spread on low-sodium bread.

PEANUT BUTTER AND TOMATO SANDWICH

Protein is important in a sodium-restricted diet. Four
tablespoons of low-sodium peanut butter supply about the
same amount of protein as two ounces of lean cooked
meat but with far fewer milligrams of sodium.

Ted had these every Saturday for weeks until I caught
onto other tasty sandwiches.

Spread unsalty's bread with low-sodium mayonnaise or
unsalted butter or margarine and low-sodium peanut butter. Add slice of tomato sprinkled with sugar and dash of
oregano. Sliced banana with nutmeg in place of tomato
is a good variety.

1 tablespoon low-sodium mayonnaise, 6 mg. sodium and 92 calories.

1 tablespoon low-sodium peanut butter, 7 mg. sodium and 100 calories.

1 banana, 1.4 mg. sodium and 99 calories.

1 tomato, 3 mg. sodium and 30 calories.

PECAN SANDWICHES

Grind pecans, moisten with low-sodium mayonnaise. Spread between unsalty's bread. Place lettuce leaf between slices.

6 whole pecans, 2.4 mg. sodium and 185 calories.

1 tablespoon low-sodium mayonnaise, 6 mg. sodium and 92 calories.

1 SERVING.

SHRIMP SANDWICH

6 *canned low-sodium shrimp, chopped*
1 *tablespoon low-sodium mayonnaise*

1 *teaspoon lemon juice*
1 *teaspoon chopped parsley*

Mix shrimp with low-sodium mayonnaise. Add lemon juice and parsley. Spread between unsalty's bread. Place lettuce leaf between slices.

4 to 6 low-sodium canned shrimp, 35 mg. sodium and 64 calories. In comparison 4 to 6 fresh shrimp, 75 mg. sodium and 64 calories. Per serving, 41 mg. sodium and 156 calories.

1 SERVING.

WATERCRESS SANDWICHES

2 tablespoons watercress, 1.3 mg. sodium and 0 calories.
1 tablespoon low-sodium mayonnaise, 6 mg. sodium and 92 calories.
1 teaspoon grated onion, 0.3 mg. sodium and 1 calorie, or 1 teaspoon chopped chives, 0.3 mg. sodium and 1 calorie.
Chopped nuts may be added. 3 walnuts, 1 mg. sodium and 78 calories.

Chop watercress, mix with unsalty's mayonnaise or butter, add grated onions or chives. Spread on low-sodium bread.
1 SERVING.

UNSALTY'S GARLIC BREAD

Spread low-sodium bread with unsalted margarine or butter. Sprinkle with garlic powder. Wrap in aluminum foil and heat in oven.
1 tablespoon unsalted margarine, 1.5 mg. sodium and 100 calories.

19 Salads, Soups, and Sauces

We should all be grateful for the salad. A salad is full of things good not only for our bodies but for our souls. A salad is pretty to look at and can change the mood of an entire meal. A colorful, attractive salad draws a meal together like a fireplace draws a magic circle. In the winter, a cold salad can make the hot dish taste hotter and in the summer a cold crisp salad can make you forget for at least a while the word "humidity."

One can make many varied dressings, but the simple dressing sometimes can be the best. Oil, vinegar, and sugar or honey are always acceptable.

Olive oil has been regarded as a basic food for thousands of years. The Phoenicians traded olive oil for gold bars. The Italians and French use it predominately in their cooking. Olive oil is unadulterated by chemicals or synthetic preservatives, so it keeps its original flavor as well as all the vitamins and mineral values of the nutritious olive. If your doctor allows olive oil, enjoy the olive in its liquid form even though you can't have the olive after man has finished putting all those things in the brine you can't have. Olive oil will keep indefinitely in the kitchen cabinet. It need not be refrigerated. Keep the container tightly capped. Do buy expensive olive oil. The flavor is so much better.

GREEN SALAD

Rub wooden salad bowl with garlic bud. Add crispy greens and sprinkle with oregano or tarragon. Mix with olive or vegetable oil and vinegar. Add a little sugar if you like.

CAESAR SALAD

No reason for unsalty not to eat Caesar salad and join the rest of the gourmets.

1 *bunch romaine*
1 *clove garlic*
4 *tablespoons olive oil*
3 *tablespoons wine vinegar*
⅛ *teaspoon dry mustard*
⅛ *teaspoon onion powder*
⅛ *teaspoon garlic powder*
1 *teaspoon sugar*
Pepper to taste
1 *beaten egg*

Rub salad bowl with garlic clove, add olive oil, vinegar, and seasonings. Stir around, then add romaine torn into medium-size pieces. Stir some more. Now add the egg and stir with salad fork and spoon. Serve a separate dish of anchovies and parmesan cheese for the salty Caesars.

8 SERVINGS. *Per serving, 10 mg. sodium and 82 calories.*

COLE SLAW

1 *cabbage*
⅓ *cup vinegar*
½ *teaspoon pepper*
¼ *teaspoon dill seed*
¼ *teaspoon tarragon*
¼ *teaspoon chervil*
4 *tablespoons sour cream*
4 *tablespoons low-sodium mayonnaise*
Paprika
Parsley

Scoop out the center section of the cabbage, leaving only a shell. Shred the center section and soak in ice water for 30 minutes. Drain and dry thoroughly, add vinegar and seasonings. Toss and let marinate for an hour. Drain again, squeezing cabbage slightly to remove any excess liquid. Pour sour cream and mayonnaise over cabbage and toss lightly. Place slaw in chilled shell of cabbage. Garnish with paprika and parsley.

8 SERVINGS. *Per serving, 14 mg. sodium and 83 calories.*

PINEAPPLE COLE SLAW

2 *cups shredded cabbage*
1 *cup crushed pineapple,*
   drained
1 *small green pepper,*
   cut fine

4 *tablespoons low-sodium*
   mayonnaise
½ *tablespoon vinegar*
⅛ *teaspoon pepper*
¼ *teaspoon dill seed*

Combine cabbage, pineapple, and green pepper. Mix well. Mix mayonnaise with vinegar, pepper, and dill seed. Combine with cabbage mixture.

6 SERVINGS. *Per serving, 9 mg. sodium and 104 calories.*

FRUIT SALAD I

3 *oranges*
3 *bananas*
15 *white grapes*
4 *slices pineapple*
2 *eggs*

¼ *cup vinegar*
1 *tablespoon water*
¼ *teaspoon dry mustard*
1 *teaspoon unsalted*
   butter or margarine

Mix orange sections, sliced bananas, grapes, and cut-up pineapple. Make dressing of well-beaten eggs, vinegar, water, mustard, and butter. Cook until thick. When cold add to fruits.

4 SERVINGS. *Per serving, 38 mg. sodium and 234 calories.*

FRUIT SALAD II

½ head lettuce
4 slices pineapple
1 can grapefruit sections
1 red apple
16 strawberries

4 tablespoons low-sodium
   mayonnaise
2 teaspoons honey
Few sprigs of mint

Line salad bowl with lettuce. Divide bowl into 4 parts with half slices of pineapple. Arrange alternate sections of grapefruit and apple, placing strawberries on top. Fill center with 4 tablespoons low-sodium mayonnaise, mixed with 2 teaspoons honey. Garnish with mint.

4 SERVINGS. *Per serving, 14 mg. sodium and 289 calories.*

FRUIT SALAD OR CUP

Use luscious fruits of the season.

2 cups sliced peeled
   ripe peaches
1 cup diced ripe pears

¾ cup fresh blueberries
¼ cup lemon juice
½ cup sugar

Mix fruit in bowl. Combine remaining ingredients, stirring to dissolve sugar. Pour over fruits, toss lightly, chill. If used for salad, serve on lettuce with low-sodium mayonnaise. A sprinkle of cinnamon, nutmeg, or cardamom is a good addition.

4 SERVINGS. *Per serving, 3 mg. sodium and 166 calories.*

FRUIT-ONION SALAD

This goes well with lamb or chicken.

Alternate slices of Valencia orange and canned cranberry sauce with thin slices of onion on a bed of lettuce. Serve with a dollop of low-sodium mayonnaise mixed with a dash of fresh lemon juice.

1 orange, 2 mg. sodium and 70 calories.

1 onion, 6 mg. sodium and 25 calories.

½ cup cranberry sauce, 1.2 mg. sodium and 274 calories.

1 tablespoon low-sodium mayonnaise, 1.5 mg. sodium and 100 calories.

APPLE SALAD

1 *apple*
½ *medium onion*
⅛ *teaspoon thyme or fennel seed*[1]

Cut apple in small cubes and cut onion fine. Add thyme or fennel seed. Serve with oil and vinegar dressing on lettuce.

1 SERVING. *Per serving (without dressing), 5 mg. sodium and 88 calories.*

---

[1] The herb fennel has a sweet licorice flavor and enhances the flavor of apples in any form.

ASTORIA SALAD
(FORMERLY KNOWN AS WALDORF)

I couldn't seem to call it Waldorf minus the celery:
anyway, the Astors should have a salad named for them.
1 apple, 2 mg. sodium and 75 calories.
*3 walnuts or pecan nuts—unsalted, 1 mg. sodium and
93 calories.*
*1 tablespoon low-sodium mayonnaise, 6 mg. sodium and
92 calories.*
⅛ teaspoon cinnamon.
Cut up apple and nuts.
Mix and serve on crisp lettuce cups.
1 SERVING.

AVOCADO CUCUMBER SALAD

Avocado or alligator pear is high in protein[2] and sometimes in Central America it takes the place of meat because of its cheapness.
Cube avocado and dice cucumbers. Season with minced
onion, lemon juice, and pepper. Serve with unsalty's low-
sodium mayonnaise on crisp lettuce.
1 avocado, 6 mg. sodium and 485 calories.
1 cucumber, 14 mg. sodium and 40 calories.
*1 tablespoon low-sodium mayonnaise, 6 mg. sodium
and 92 calories.*

POTATO SALAD

Make this an hour or so before serving. Gives the herbs
a chance to meld.

---

[2] Calories too!

4 *medium-size new potatoes*
1 *medium chopped onion*
1 *tablespoon chopped green pepper*
¼ *cup diced cucumber*
1 *hard cooked egg, chopped*
4 *slices low-sodium cucumber pickles*

1 *tablespoon fresh chopped parsley*
½ *teaspoon rosemary*
¼ *teaspoon celery seed*
½ *teaspoon oregano*
⅛ *teaspoon garlic powder*
Pepper to taste
4 *tablespoons low-sodium mayonnaise*
1 *tablespoon vinegar or dry white wine*

Cook new potatoes whole in skins, peel, and dice. Mix potatoes with onion, green pepper, cucumber, egg, pickles, parsley, rosemary, celery seed, oregano, garlic powder, and pepper. Mix mayonnaise and vinegar or wine, add to potato mixture. Mix well. Chill salad thoroughly.

6 SERVINGS. *Per serving, 20 mg. sodium and 148 calories.*

CHICKEN SALAD

1¼ *cups diced, unsalted, white cooked chicken*
1 *large diced apple*
4 *slices pineapple, cut in pieces*

2 *tablespoons low-sodium mayonnaise*
½ *teaspoon curry powder*
⅛ *cup chopped unsalted almonds*

Combine ingredients, serve on lettuce cups, and top with dash of curry powder.

4 SERVINGS. *Per serving, 59 mg. sodium and 252 calories.*

CHICKEN SALAD WITH
SOUR-CREAM DRESSING

2 cups diced unsalted
   white chicken
½ cup sour cream
2 tablespoons dry sherry

¼ teaspoon dry mustard
1 apple, diced
¼ cup blanched unsalted
   almonds, slivered

Mix and serve on lettuce or watercress.

4 SERVINGS. *Per serving, 104 mg. sodium and 356 calories.*

SHRIMP SALAD

12 low-sodium canned
   shrimp, cut up
1 tablespoon dry white
   wine
1 teaspoon chopped
   parsley

1 teaspoon lemon juice
1 tablespoon low-sodium
   mayonnaise

Soak shrimp in wine for ½ hour. Remove shrimp and mix with other ingredients. Serve on lettuce leaves.

1 SERVING. *Per serving, 74 mg. sodium and 231 calories.*

ALASKA SALAD MOLD

Welcome our fiftieth state!

1 cup canned low-sodium
   or fresh-cooked salmon
½ cup finely chopped
   cucumber
¼ cup minced onion
¼ cup low-sodium catsup
⅛ cup vinegar

1 tablespoon unflavored
   gelatin
¼ cup cold water
½ cup low-sodium
   mayonnaise
Tomatoes or lemons
Parsley

Drain flaked salmon, reserve liquid. Mix with cucumber and onion. Combine reserved salmon liquid, catsup, and vinegar. Bring to boil. Add gelatin softened in water and stir until dissolved. Blend hot liquid with salmon mixture. Stir in mayonnaise. Stir into oiled mold. Chill. Garnish with tomatoes or lemons and parsley.

4 SERVINGS. *Per serving, 45 mg. sodium and 260 calories.*

BING CHERRY MOLD

Delicious. Makes one think of cherry-blossom time and a drive through the country to see the orchards.

1 *cup canned bing cherries*	½ *cup sugar*
1 *cup cherry juice*	1 *tablespoon lemon juice*
¾ *cup sherry wine*	1½ *tablespoons*
1 *cup orange juice*	*unflavored gelatin*

Dissolve gelatin in ½ cup orange juice. Bring cherry juice and remaining orange juice to boil, add gelatin mixture, sugar, sherry and lemon juice. Mix until dissolved. Add cherries. Pour in mold and chill.

6 SERVINGS. *Per serving, 7 mg. sodium and 164 calories.*

CRANBERRY ASPIC

Aspic means a savory jelly and this lives up to the meaning.

1 *envelope unflavored*	½ *cup tangerine juice*
gelatin	¼ *cup apple juice*
1½ *cups cranberry juice*	¼ *cup ginger ale*
cocktail	

Soften gelatin in ½ cup cold cranberry juice. Heat one

cup of the cocktail to boiling point. Add softened gelatin and dissolve. Stir in other ingredients. Pour into lightly oiled molds, chill until firm.

6 SERVINGS. *Per serving, 3 mg. sodium and 66 calories.*

CRANBERRY RING SALAD

When you serve cold turkey, this is a must.

2 *cups cranberries*   1 *tablespoon unflavored*
1½ *cups cold water*   *gelatin*
1 *cup sugar*   ½ *cup chopped walnuts*
⅛ *teaspoon mace*

Wash cranberries, add 1 cup cold water, cook until tender. Add sugar and mace and cook 5 minutes. Soften gelatin in ½ cup cold water, dissolve in hot cranberries. Chill until mixture begins to thicken. Add nuts, mix. Pour into oiled mold. Chill until firm.

6 SERVINGS. *Per serving, 2 mg. sodium and 213 calories.*

GRAPEFRUIT RING

This is full of Vitamin C and alkalines.

2½ *tablespoons*   1 *cup hot water*
  unflavored gelatin   1½ *cups grapefruit juice*
½ *cup cold water*   ½ *cup orange juice*
1½ *cups sugar*   ¼ *cup lemon juice*

Soften gelatin in cold water 5 minutes. Boil sugar and hot water 3 minutes or until clear. Pour over softened gelatin and stir until dissolved. Cool and add grapefruit, orange, and lemon juice and pour into ring mold. Chill.

8 SERVINGS. *Per serving, 3 mg. sodium and 184 calories.*

GRAPEFRUIT CUCUMBER SALAD

1 *envelope unflavored gelatin*
⅔ *cup grapefruit juice*
1 *tablespoon lime juice*
1 *teaspoon vinegar*
1¼ *cups grapefruit sections*

2 *cups drained grated cucumber*
1 *cup low-sodium cottage cheese*
½ *cup low-sodium mayonnaise*
¼ *cup minced parsley*
Watercress or lettuce

Soften gelatin in grapefruit syrup. Heat, stirring constantly until gelatin dissolves. Add lime juice and vinegar. Combine grapefruit sections, cucumber, cottage cheese, low-sodium mayonnaise, and parsley. Add to gelatin mixture and blend. Spoon into molds. Chill until firm. Serve on watercress or lettuce.

6 SERVINGS. *Per serving, 23 mg. sodium and 230 calories.*

PUREE OF AVOCADO SOUP

Appetizing soups were most difficult to prepare without salt. I tried and tried, and wasted and wasted. These few are *good*.

2 *avocados*
1 *tablespoon lemon juice*
¼ *teaspoon paprika*
2 *teaspoons chopped chives*
1 *teaspoon grated lemon rind*

¼ *teaspoon dill, ground*
¼ *teaspoon oregano*
2 *teaspoons grated onions*
2 *cups milk*

Peel, seed, and mash avocados. Add rest of the ingredients. Heat in double boiler. This is a thick soup, and can also be made with low-sodium dry milk if you wish to cut the count.

4 SERVINGS. *Per serving, 64 mg. sodium and 326 calories.*

BEEF BROTH

Old-fashioned beef broth tastes good. Measure allowed ounces of lean ground beef and add water to cover. Simmer slowly 15 minutes. Season with garlic or onion powder, parsley and a little lemon juice. Pepper to taste.

HOT YOGURT BEEF SOUP

1½ cups yogurt
4 low-sodium bouillon
  cubes mixed with
  4 cups boiling water
3 tablespoons unsalted
  butter or margarine

¾ cup flour
½ tablespoon dried mint
  leaves
Pepper to taste

Put yogurt in mixing bowl, add stock slowly, stirring to smooth consistency. Melt butter or margarine in saucepan. Add flour slowly, stirring constantly over low flame. Then add yogurt and stock mixture gradually, stirring constantly until it boils. Pour into soup bowls and top with dried mint leaves. Season with pepper.

6 SERVINGS. *Per serving, 51 mg. sodium and 137 calories.*

CONSOMME JULIENNE

1 tablespoon unsalted
  butter or margarine
1 cup julienne carrot
  strips
½ cup julienne leek
  strips
½ cup finely shredded
  cabbage
¼ cup thin onion slices

Pepper to taste
1 teaspoon sugar
¼ teaspoon basil
¼ teaspoon dill, ground
3 low-sodium bouillon
  cubes dissolved in
  3 cups boiling water
Parsley, chopped

Melt butter or margarine in saucepan, add vegetables, seasonings, and sugar. Cover. Cook over low heat for 5 minutes or until vegetables are tender. Add bouillon mixture. Simmer 5 minutes. Serve garnished with chopped parsley. If calories permit, add 1 tablespoon sour cream when consommé is served.

4 SERVINGS. *Per serving (without sour cream), 41 mg. sodium and 57 calories.*

ORANGE SOUP

I never knew one could make soup out of orange juice. You can, and it's delicious.

2 cups orange juice
1 tablespoon lemon juice
½ cup sugar
½ cup water
⅛ teaspoon allspice
Small stick cinnamon

¾ teaspoon grated orange
  rind
1½ teaspoons cornstarch
¼ cup water
Fresh mint

Mix together the first 7 ingredients, boil 5 minutes. Blend cornstarch and the remaining ¼ cup water. Stir into hot juice mixture. Boil 5 minutes, stirring constantly. Remove cinnamon. Chill. Garnish with fresh mint.

3 SERVINGS. *Per serving, 4 mg. sodium and 206 calories.*

TOMATO BOUILLON

4 *cups canned low-sodium*
    tomato juice
½ *bay leaf*
2 *cloves*
¼ *teaspoon dill seed*
¼ *teaspoon basil*
¼ *teaspoon marjoram*

¼ *teaspoon oregano*
½ *teaspoon sugar*
Pepper to taste
2 *teaspoons unsalted*
    butter or margarine
    or sour cream
Parsley, chopped

Combine ingredients. Let stand 1 hour. Heat to boiling point, strain. Pour into serving bowls, add per serving ½ teaspoon butter or margarine or sour cream. Garnish with parsley. Dash of curry adds flavor.

4 SERVINGS. *Per serving, 12 mg. sodium and 74 calories.*

TOMATO SOUP

½ *cup finely chopped*
    onion
1 *tablespoon unsalted*
    butter or margarine
2 *cups canned low-sodium*
    tomatoes

2 *tablespoons white wine*
¼ *teaspoon ground dill*
¼ *teaspoon basil*
1 *tablespoon chopped*
    parsley
1 *tablespoon sour cream*

Sauté onion in butter or margarine until tender. Add tomatoes, wine, dill, basil, and parsley. Simmer 20 minutes. Pour into serving dishes and top with sour cream.

2 SERVINGS. *Per serving, 22 mg. sodium and 142 calories.*

For a heartier soup, ground cooked lean beef may be added.

3 *oz. cooked beef, 80 mg. sodium and 250 calories.*

WATERCRESS SOUP

1 *bunch watercress,*	½ *teaspoon rosemary*
washed and chopped	1 *egg yolk*
4 *large potatoes*	*Juice of 1 lemon*
Pepper to taste	*Paprika*
½ *teaspoon sage*	*Parsley*

Boil the potatoes until ¾ done. Add watercress, pepper. Mash and strain through sieve. Put back into saucepan with enough of the potato water to make a soup. Add sage and rosemary. Cook 20 minutes without boiling. Beat the egg yolk into the lemon juice and add slowly to the soup. Garnish with paprika and parsley.

6 SERVINGS. *Per serving, 9 mg. sodium and 74 calories.*

COLD YOGURT SOUP
(Unsalty's Vichyssoise)

This is a Turkish recipe. If you were dining in Istanbul, your host would greet you with the pre-meal salutation, "May it give you good health."

1 *pint yogurt*	2 *tablespoons olive oil*
3 *medium cucumbers*	1 *tablespoon chopped*
1 *clove garlic*	*fresh mint or ½*
1 *tablespoon vinegar*	*teaspoon dried mint*
1 *teaspoon dill,*[3] *ground*	*leaves*
3 *tablespoons water*	

Peel cucumbers, quarter lengthwise, and slice about ⅛ inch thick. Place in bowl. Rub another bowl with garlic and swish vinegar around to collect flavor, then add dill,

---

[3] Dill (seed or ground) is a fine herb to experiment with. Try dill with soups, meats, fish, sour cream, peas, cabbage, cauliflower, string beans, and macaroni.

water, and yogurt. Stir until mixture is smooth. Pour over cucumbers and stir again. Pour into serving dishes. Sprinkle with olive oil and garnish with mint.

4 SERVINGS. *Per serving, 69 mg. sodium and 153 calories.*

UNSALTY'S FRENCH DRESSING

½ cup olive or other
 vegetable oil
1¾ teaspoons paprika
1 teaspoon dry mustard
1½ garlic cloves
½ teaspoon basil
⅛ teaspoon pepper

1 tablespoon chopped
 onions or chives
3 tablespoons cider
 vinegar
2 tablespoons lemon juice
2 teaspoons chopped
 fresh parsley

Combine all ingredients. Let sit in covered jar in refrigerator at least 12 hours before serving. Shake before using.

Total recipe, 4 mg. sodium and 1017 calories. Per tablespoon, negligible sodium and 78 calories.

LOW-SODIUM MAYONNAISE[4]

This homemade low-sodium mayonnaise has much less sodium than most standard commercial low-sodium preparations, but in counting the sodium content for mayonnaise in other recipes, I used the milligrams for the higher count commercial low-sodium mayonnaise.

1 egg yolk
Few grains cayenne
½ teaspoon mustard
½ teaspoon sugar

1¼ tablespoons vinegar
¾ tablespoon lemon juice
1 cup olive or other
 vegetable oil

[4] Dressings, sauces and bastings are wonderful additions to unsalty's diet, but they do add calories. Use them with care if you need to watch your weight.

Place egg yolk in a deep bowl. Mix cayenne, mustard, and sugar. Stir mixture into egg yolk. Stir in vinegar and lemon juice, add drop or two of oil. Beat with fork or egg beater until thoroughly mixed. Continue adding the oil, a few drops at a time, beating vigorously after each addition until about ¼ of the oil has been used. A wire whisk is wonderful for making mayonnaise. Beat in remaining oil, 1 or 2 tablespoons at a time. Add more vinegar or lemon juice if too thick. Mayonnaise thickens as it stands, but if too thick will separate on standing. Store in covered jar in refrigerator or cool place.

MAKES 1¼ CUPS. *Total recipe, 15 mg. sodium and 2078 calories. Per tablespoon, negligible sodium and 104 calories.*

EGGLESS MAYONNAISE

½ teaspoon confectioners'
  sugar
¼ teaspoon dry mustard
¼ teaspoon paprika
Few grains cayenne
1 tablespoon vinegar

1 tablespoon lemon juice
¼ cup chilled
  evaporated milk
1 cup chilled olive or
  vegetable oil

Beat first 7 ingredients until well blended. Add ⅓ cup oil and beat. Add remaining oil and beat again.

MAKES 1½ CUPS. *Total recipe, 62 mg. sodium and 2092 calories. Per tablespoon, 3 mg. sodium and 86 calories.*

LOW-SODIUM COTTAGE CHEESE
SALAD DRESSING

The first week my husband was on his diet I bought low-sodium cottage cheese. Have you ever tasted it? Do —then try this recipe. Serve with fruit or vegetable salad.

1 cup low-sodium cottage
  cheese
¼ cup diced fresh
  tomatoes or ½ apple
  cut up fine
1 teaspoon sugar
½ teaspoon vinegar

½ teaspoon paprika
Few grains cayenne
¼ teaspoon allspice
½ teaspoon dill, ground
⅛ teaspoon garlic powder
⅛ teaspoon caraway seed

Combine all ingredients and mix well. Moisten with low-sodium mayonnaise if you wish. A good addition is two tablespoons of sour cream.

MAKES 1¼ CUPS. *Total recipe (including sour cream), 62 mg. sodium and 374 calories. Per tablespoon, 3 mg. sodium and 19 calories.*

TED'S FAVORITE DRESSING

¼ cup honey
¼ cup olive oil

¼ cup wine or cider
  vinegar
Clove garlic

Place in covered jar, shake well, store in refrigerator. *Total recipe, 26 mg. sodium (with wine vinegar) and 756 calories. Total recipe, 6 mg. sodium (with cider vinegar) and 756 calories. Per tablespoon, 2 mg. sodium (with wine vinegar) and 72 calories. Per tablespoon, negligible sodium (with cider vinegar) and 63 calories.*

SPECIAL RUSSIAN DRESSING

4 tablespoons low-sodium
  mayonnaise
1 tablespoon low-sodium
  catsup

1 teaspoon tarragon
  vinegar
1 teaspoon chives,
  chopped

Mix, chill, and serve.

Total recipe, 31 mg. sodium and 385 calories. Per table-spoon, 6 mg. sodium and 77 calories.

APPLE SALAD DRESSING

2 tablespoons low-sodium mayonnaise

2 teaspoons concentrated frozen orange juice

Beat until blended.

Total recipe, 13 mg. sodium and 196 calories. Per table-spoon, 5 mg. sodium and 73 calories.

FRUIT SALAD DRESSING I

1 cup powdered sugar

¾ cup vinegar (cider)

¾ cup vegetable oil

1 teaspoon grated onion

Boil sugar and vinegar 5 minutes. Stir, let cool. Beat in oil with electric mixer, add onion. A dash of curry may be added. Refreshing with fresh fruit.

Total recipe, 18 mg. sodium and 2020 calories. Per tablespoon, negligible sodium and 50 calories.

FRUIT SALAD DRESSING II

1 cup grapefruit juice

3 tablespoons olive or vegetable oil

Whip with egg beater and chill.

Total recipe, 4 mg. sodium and 505 calories. Per table-spoon, negligible sodium and 26 calories.

QUICK FRUIT GLAZE

Try this over peaches for dessert or as a sauce for cold meats.

Heat ½ cup currant jelly until it melts. Spoon over fruit.

Total recipe, 8 mg. sodium and 440 calories. Per tablespoon, 1 mg. sodium and 55 calories.

NOT SO QUICK FRUIT GLAZE

3 *cups sugar*   ¾ *cup fruit juice*
1 *tablespoon cornstarch*

Combine sugar and cornstarch in pan, add fruit juice. Heat and stir until liquid is thick and clear. Remove from heat. When almost cold, pour over fruit.

Total recipe, 7 mg. sodium and 3190 calories. Per tablespoon, negligible sodium and 100 calories.

HERB BUTTER FOR BASTING
FISH OR CHICKEN

2 *tablespoons unsalted*   ⅛ *teaspoon dry mustard*
  butter or margarine   1 *tablespoon chopped*
¼ *teaspoon lemon juice*   *parsley or chives*

Beat butter until soft. Add rest of ingredients and mix well.

2 SERVINGS. Total recipe, 4 mg. sodium and 203 calories.

HERB BUTTER FOR FISH

This may be used on any fish to be baked or broiled.

Combine:

¼ cup unsalted butter
  or margarine
1 teaspoon grated onion
½ teaspoon lemon juice
½ teaspoon rosemary

½ teaspoon tarragon
½ teaspoon chopped
  parsley
Pepper to taste

4 SERVINGS. *Total recipe, 6 mg. sodium and 404 calories.*

OYSTER SAUCE

½ cup white wine vinegar
3 teaspoons black ground
  pepper

3 shallots, chopped fine
Few grains cayenne

Combine ingredients. Store covered in refrigerator 3 days. Serve cold with oysters.
Total recipe, 43 mg. sodium and 27 calories.

BASTING SAUCE FOR BROILERS

2 tablespoons melted
  unsalted butter or
  margarine

2 tablespoons sherry
½ teaspoon paprika
¼ teaspoon rosemary

Combine ingredients and use to baste chicken while broiling.
Total recipe, 8 mg. sodium and 244 calories.

LEMON BASTING SAUCE FOR TURKEY OR CHICKEN

Melt ¾ cup unsalted butter or margarine.
Mix and stir into melted butter or margarine the following:

2 teaspoons paprika	¼ teaspoon dry mustard
1 teaspoon sugar	Few grains cayenne
½ teaspoon black pepper	pepper

Blend in thoroughly:

½ cup lemon juice	2 teaspoons grated onion
½ cup hot water	

Baste chicken frequently with sauce during grilling of chicken breasts. Start the chicken cooking with the inside facing down, basting frequently with lemon sauce. Breasts will take 30 minutes or so depending on size. Use sauce for basting roast turkey or chicken.
Total recipe, 24 mg. sodium and 1246 calories.

CHERRY CHICKEN BASTE

1 8-oz. jar cherry	¼ teaspoon allspice
preserves	¼ cup unsalted butter
1 tablespoon vinegar	or margarine
4 cloves	

Heat and baste broiled or roast chicken.
Total recipe, 22 mg. sodium and 1282 calories.

PEACH JUICE TURKEY BASTE

¼ cup unsalted butter
or margarine
¼ cup sherry wine or
apple juice

2 cups canned peach
juice

Melt butter or margarine, add wine or apple juice and peach juice. Use peaches filled with cranberry sauce for garnish.

Total recipe (with wine), 32 mg. sodium and 692 calories.

CUCUMBER SAUCE

Try this with cold salmon.

1 medium cucumber
1 tablespoon vinegar
⅛ teaspoon pepper

Few grains cayenne
1 teaspoon minced onion

Peel the cucumber, chop very fine, add remaining ingredients. Add ½ cup sour cream if you can afford the count and calories.

Total recipe (without sour cream), 15 mg. sodium and 42 calories.

JELLY SAUCE

½ teaspoon dry mustard
⅛ teaspoon ground cloves
⅛ teaspoon cinnamon

1 tablespoon vinegar
½ cup currant jelly

Combine all ingredients in a saucepan. Cook over low

heat, stirring constantly until jelly is melted. Serve hot with meat or vegetables.

Total recipe, 8 mg. sodium and 442 calories. Per tablespoon, 1 mg. sodium and 54 calories.

MUSTARD SAUCE

1 *tablespoon low-sodium*   1 *teaspoon low-sodium*
  mayonnaise   *prepared mustard*
2 *teaspoons sour cream*

Combine ingredients. Mix well. Serve with cold meats and vegetables.

1 SERVING. *Total recipe, 13 mg. sodium and 157 calories.*

SOUR CREAM AND WINE SAUCE

½ *cup sour cream*   ½ *teaspoon nutmeg*
2 *tablespoons sherry*

Blend. Serve with soups, puddings, chilled fruit, vegetables, or meat.

Total recipe, 50 mg. sodium and 436 calories. Per tablespoon, 5 mg. sodium and 43 calories.

SAUCE PIQUANT

Good with cold meats and fowl.

1 *cup red wine or dry*   2 *cloves garlic, chopped*
  sauterne   ¼ *cup wine vinegar*
1 *cup olive oil*   ⅛ *teaspoon dried red*
2 *chopped onions*   *pepper*
⅛ *teaspoon rosemary*

Mix all ingredients thoroughly, stir until well blended. Put in jar to marinate for 24 hours. Remove garlic. May be used to baste meats and fowl while roasting or broiling. Exotic flavor.

Total recipe, 53 mg. sodium and 2225 calories. Per tablespoon, 2 mg. sodium and 62 calories.

STEAK MARINADE

Cooking over charcoal gives meat and poultry a wonderful flavor, and seasonings are not really necessary as they are in other methods of cooking. Try this marinade. Everyone will enjoy the flavor.

1 cup red wine
½ cup olive or vegetable oil
⅓ cup brown sugar
¼ teaspoon marjoram
¼ teaspoon rosemary
2 large onions, thinly sliced
1 clove garlic, minced

Combine all ingredients and mix well. Allow steak to marinate at least 4 hours or, better yet, overnight.

Total recipe, 40 mg. sodium and 1489 calories.

CHICKEN MARINADE

½ cup olive or vegetable oil
3 tablespoons white vinegar
½ teaspoon pepper
2 teaspoons minced parsley
½ teaspoon rosemary
½ teaspoon tarragon
½ teaspoon basil
1 clove garlic

Combine all ingredients and mix well. Marinate for 2 hours at room temperature.

Total recipe, 16 mg. sodium and 1006 calories.

VANILLA SAUCE

¼ cup sugar
1 tablespoon cornstarch
1 cup water

2 tablespoons unsalted
   butter or margarine
1 teaspoon vanilla

Combine sugar, cornstarch, and water. Heat until thickened, about 5 minutes. Remove from flame and stir in butter or margarine and vanilla. Chill.

Total recipe, 4 mg. sodium and 422 calories. Per tablespoon, negligible sodium and 22 calories.

HARD SAUCE

Serve this on pumpkin pie or baked apples.

4 tablespoons unsalted
   butter or margarine
2 cups confectioners'
   sugar

1 egg
½ teaspoon vanilla
1 tablespoon sherry or
   brandy

Cream butter or margarine, sugar, and egg. Add flavorings, beat until creamy. Chill.

Total recipe, 79 mg. sodium and 1509 calories. Per tablespoon, 2 mg. sodium and 43 calories.

UNSALTY'S PICKLES

You can make your own pickles by boiling up a little dill, pickling spice, sugar and white vinegar and then pouring over sliced cucumbers that have been placed in a jar. Cover, cool and refrigerate.

Mg. sodium negligible.

CRANBERRY-ORANGE RELISH

To see the cranberry bogs in the fall of the year at Cape Cod is a lasting memory.

4 *cups cranberries*
  (1 lb.)
2 *oranges, quartered*
  (seeds removed)

2 *cups sugar*
¼ *teaspoon allspice*

Put cranberries and oranges (rind too) through the food grinder (coarse blade). Stir in sugar and allspice and chill. Wonderful with all meats. Keeps for weeks in refrigerator. Makes 2 pints. Allspice goes with all cranberry dishes.

Total recipe, 10 mg. sodium and 1896 calories. Per tablespoon, negligible sodium and 29 calories.

SWEET PEPPER RELISH

Who says unsalty can't have a relish?

6 *red peppers* (*not the*
  hot variety)
6 *green peppers*

6 *small onions* (*peeled*)
1 *cup mild cider vinegar*
¾ *cup sugar*

Put peppers and onions through meat grinder. Cover with boiling water and let stand 10 minutes. Drain. Combine remaining ingredients and boil for 5 minutes. Add vegetables and boil 10 minutes. Store in refrigerator.

Total recipe, 24 mg. sodium and 847 calories. Per tablespoon, negligible sodium and 9 calories.

20 Meat, Morsels, and Manna

And the House of Israel called the name thereof manna: and it was like coriander seed, white: and the taste of it was like wafers made with honey.

EXODUS 16:31

Beef

Beef has a wonderful natural flavor, and lemon juice helps to bring out the flavor. Try rubbing steak with lemon juice, garlic, and ginger. When cooking a roast of beef, rub with garlic and freshly ground black pepper. Cook cube steaks with chopped green pepper and onions or chives and a sprinkle of oregano. Do read the recipes for sauces to serve with leftover beef.

MEAT LOAF

1½ lbs. ground lean beef
1 medium onion,
  chopped fine
½ cup wheat germ or
  low-sodium bread
  crumbs
1 cup canned low-sodium
  tomatoes
1 egg
2 teaspoons chopped
  parsley

1 tablespoon olive or
  vegetable oil
1 teaspoon basil
1 teaspoon oregano
1 teaspoon sugar
⅛ teaspoon garlic
  powder
¼ teaspoon allspice
¼ teaspoon pepper
1 tablespoon chopped
  green pepper

Mix ingredients thoroughly. I use my clean hands. Bake at 350 degrees for 1 to 1¼ hours.

6 SERVINGS. *Per serving, 95 mg. sodium and 319 calories.*

APPLESAUCE AND MEAT LOAF

Many think the herb "allspice" combines the flavor of cloves, cinnamon, and nutmeg. It comes from the small fruit of an evergreen of the myrtle family.

1½ lbs. ground lean beef
1 egg, beaten
2 tablespoons chopped
  onion

1 teaspoon allspice
1 cup applesauce

Combine ingredients. Pack into a greased loaf pan.

The Topping

1 pared apple cut in
  rings
¼ cup brown sugar

1 teaspoon mustard
1 tablespoon water
⅛ teaspoon cloves

Press apple rings on top of loaf. Mix sugar, cloves, water, and mustard and pour on top. Bake at 350 degrees for 1 hour and 15 minutes.

8 SERVINGS. *Per serving, 95 mg. sodium and 339 calories.*

SWEDISH MEATBALLS

1 *lb. ground round beef*	1 *teaspoon brown sugar*
½ *lb. ground pork*	¼ *teaspoon pepper*
½ *tablespoon minced onions*	½ *teaspoon nutmeg*
1 *tablespoon vegetable oil*	½ *teaspoon cloves*
1 *beaten egg*	½ *teaspoon ginger*
½ *cup wheat germ or low-sodium bread crumbs or low-sodium cornflakes*	½ *teaspoon allspice*
	2 *cups boiling water*

Fry onions. Mix all ingredients with onions, form into small balls, brown well in onion fat. Cover with boiling water and simmer meatballs, covered, for 20 to 30 minutes. Remove meatballs to warm casserole.

Gravy

2 *cups stock*	4 *teaspoons lemon juice*
2 *tablespoons flour*	

Pour off all but 4 tablespoons of the stock into another pan. Blend in flour. Stir the gravy until thick. Add rest of stock, slowly, stirring constantly. Add lemon juice. Pour over meatballs.

6 SERVINGS. *Per serving, 87 mg. sodium and 323 calories.*

HERBED HAMBURGERS

I can't understand why anybody eats hamburgers any other way, or why somebody doesn't start a roadside stand and put up a big sign, "Charcoal-Herbed Hamburgers."

2 lbs. ground lean beef	1 tablespoon chopped fresh parsley
1 tablespoon olive oil or unsalted butter or margarine	¼ teaspoon marjoram
½ cup finely chopped onion	¼ teaspoon basil
	2 tablespoons lemon juice
½ teaspoon garlic powder or 1 clove minced garlic	2 teaspoons cold water

Mix all ingredients and make patties. Broil, charcoal-broil, or pan fry. A chopped tomato may be added to mixture. We like it. Makes 10 hamburgers.

Per hamburger, 65 mg. sodium and 214 calories.

HAMBURGER WITH RED WINE

1 lb. ground lean beef	¼ teaspoon marjoram
¼ cup red wine	2 tablespoons unsalted butter or margarine
1 teaspoon low-sodium Worcestershire sauce	1 onion, minced

Mix wine with Worcestershire sauce and marjoram. Make eight small patties. Brown the patties in butter or margarine. Sprinkle onion on top of each patty and spoon sauce over each. Cook until done to your choosing.

4 SERVINGS. *Per serving, 85 mg. sodium and 316 calories.*

BEEF STEW

A dull name for a dish we have so enjoyed. Buy a glamorous French earthenware dish to serve the stew, and it will compensate for the name.

2 lbs. lean beef, cubed
3 tablespoons unsalted butter or margarine
1 tablespoon flour
6 oz. white wine
4 tomatoes, cut and diced
10 small new onions
2 bay leaves

6 whole cloves
½ teaspoon allspice
Freshly ground black pepper to taste
1½ cups boiling water
½ cup carrots, cut into olive shapes
10 small new potatoes

Sauté beef in butter or margarine until golden brown, add flour, wine, tomatoes, onions, and seasonings. Cover with water. Cook over low flame 2½ hours. Add carrots and potatoes. Simmer ½ hour longer.

6 SERVINGS. *3 oz. cooked beef, with all ingredients, 94 mg. sodium and 397 calories.*

BEEF GOULASH

Wouldn't this be good when snow is on the ground?

1½ lbs. lean stewing beef, cubed
¾ cup chopped onion
¼ cup unsalted butter or margarine
1½ teaspoons caraway seed
½ teaspoon marjoram

2 garlic cloves, minced
2 cups water
1½ tablespoons paprika
4 tablespoons low-sodium catsup
2 tablespoons water
6 boiled potatoes (hot)

Sauté onion in butter or margarine for 5 minutes. Add beef, caraway, marjoram, garlic, and water. Bring to a boil, reduce heat, cover, and simmer for 1 hour. Combine paprika, catsup, and 2 tablespoons of water. Add this mixture to the stew and simmer for 10 minutes. Serve with potatoes.

6 SERVINGS. *Per serving, 88 mg. sodium and 429 calories.*

OLD-FASHIONED BEEF POT ROAST

All families like a good old-fashioned pot roast.

3 *lbs. lean beef*	1½ *tablespoons*
1 *tablespoon flour*	*vegetable oil*
¼ *teaspoon ground*	1 *pint boiling water*
pepper	2 *onions*
½ *teaspoon allspice*	2 *cloves*

Mix the flour with pepper and allspice and dredge meat with the mixture. Melt the oil in a heavy pan. (If you don't have an iron kettle, ask for one for your birthday.) Brown meat on all sides, add the boiling water, onions, and cloves, cover and allow to simmer for about 3 hours or until meat is tender. One half hour before meat is finished, potatoes may be added.

6 SERVINGS. *3 oz. cooked beef with all ingredients, 82 mg. sodium and 285 calories.*

POT ROAST WITH BURGUNDY

4 lbs. pot roast
1 garlic bud
Pepper to taste
¼ cup flour
¼ teaspoon basil
3 tablespoons olive or
    vegetable oil
½ cup canned
    low-sodium tomatoes
    (fresh tomatoes may
    be used)

3 onions, quartered
1 cup water
¾ cup burgundy
3 potatoes, quartered
1 carrot, finely cut

Rub roast with garlic and pepper. Mix flour with basil and rub surface of meat. Brown meat in oil in iron pot or the roasting pan you like. Add tomatoes, onions, water, and wine. Cover and cook on top of stove 3½ to 4 hours. Add potatoes and carrot last hour of cooking. Red table wine may be substituted for burgundy.

8 SERVINGS. *3 oz. cooked beef with all ingredients, 92 mg. sodium and 392 calories (burgundy) or 377 calories (red table wine).*

POT ROAST OF BEEF COOKED WITH PRUNE JUICE

4 lbs. pot roast
2 tablespoons flour
½ teaspoon pepper
2 tablespoons olive or
    vegetable oil

1½ cups prune juice
4 cloves
1 bay leaf
½ teaspoon thyme
8 whole prunes

Rub meat with flour and pepper. Heat the oil in large heavy kettle (the kind I have planted with geraniums), add meat, and brown on all sides. Add prune juice, cloves, bay leaf, thyme, and prunes. Cover tightly and simmer 3 to 4 hours. Turn the meat occasionally. Add more prune juice if necessary. Thicken liquid with a little flour for gravy.

8 SERVINGS. *3 oz. cooked beef with all ingredients, 83 mg. sodium and 349 calories.*

POT ROAST WITH TOMATOES

Have this a lot.

2 *lbs. round steak*
1 *tablespoon olive or vegetable oil*
1 *chopped onion*
2 *cups hot water*
1 *cup canned low-sodium tomatoes*

½ *teaspoon basil*
1 *tablespoon sugar*
1 *slice lemon*
1 *teaspoon allspice*

Brown meat in oil, add onions and hot water, then add other ingredients. Simmer slowly for 3 hours.

6 SERVINGS. *Per serving, 110 mg. sodium and 374 calories.*

BEEF BURGUNDY

3 *lbs. lean round steak cut in ½-inch cubes*
3 *tablespoons flour*
¼ *teaspoon pepper*
½ *cup unsalted butter or margarine*
2 *medium onions, chopped fine*
½ *cup leeks or scallions, chopped coarse*

½ *cup carrots, sliced*
1 *tablespoon fresh parsley, chopped*
1 *tablespoon chives, minced*
1 *clove garlic, crushed*
2 *tablespoons cognac*
1½ *cups burgundy wine*

Dredge meat in flour and pepper. Sauté in hot butter or margarine until very brown. Transfer meat, drained, to casserole. Add vegetables and garlic to remaining fat in skillet, brown lightly, stirring constantly. Flame cognac in a soup ladle and pour over beef. Add seasonings and vegetables. Pour over enough wine to cover casserole. Bake at 350 degrees for 3 hours. Serve with parsley potato or buttered noodles. Make day before if you like.

8 SERVINGS. *3 oz. cooked beef with all ingredients, 91 mg. sodium and 464 calories (burgundy) or 423 calories (red table wine).*

ESTOUFADE OF BEEF

Susan worked hours on this and was crushed when our guests liked the good "stew."

½ lb. pea beans	4 tomatoes, finely chopped
1 bay leaf	2 onions, finely chopped
½ teaspoon cumin	2 carrots, finely chopped
2 lbs. round steak, cut in 6 pieces	Pepper to taste
	1 clove garlic
2 tablespoons unsalted butter or margarine	½ teaspoon thyme
	½ teaspoon marjoram
2 cups red wine	2 tablespoons cornstarch

Cook beans with bay leaf and cumin according to directions on package but *without* salt. In a heavy pot, brown beef in butter or margarine. Add wine, vegetables, and seasonings. Cover and simmer for 2 to 2½ hours or until tender. You might need to add a little more wine mixed with water. Place beef over beans on platter. Strain liquid into a saucepan, thicken with cornstarch mixed with a little water. Pour sauce over beef.

6 SERVINGS. *3 oz. cooked beef with all ingredients, 103 mg. sodium and 494 calories.*

STEW IN A RUSH

That was the name of the original recipe because of the use of canned vegetables. These are fresh vegetables, so it is a little less of a rush.

2 lbs. ground lean beef	2 tablespoons flour
2 tablespoons onion, chopped	¾ cup sliced carrots
	1 tablespoon vegetable oil
¼ cup sherry	1 cup water
1 tablespoon dry mustard	8 sliced mushrooms
½ teaspoon thyme	18 small white onions
¼ teaspoon pepper	

Thoroughly combine first 6 ingredients, shape in walnut-size meat balls (about 30). Dust lightly with flour and brown on all sides in hot oil (about 10 minutes). Add cooked carrots, mushrooms, and onions with water. Cover and heat through.

6 SERVINGS. *Per serving, 122 mg. sodium and 402 calories.*

SAUERBRATEN

4 lbs. beef pot roast	8 whole cloves
2 cups vinegar	1 medium onion, sliced
2 cups water	2 tablespoons flour
3 bay leaves	2 tablespoons vegetable oil
10 peppercorns	

Combine vinegar, water, bay leaves, peppercorns, cloves, and onion. Bring to boil. Place meat in bowl. Pour hot mixture over meat. Cover and marinate in refrigerator for 2 days. Turn occasionally. Remove meat, drain, and rub with flour. Brown on all sides in hot oil. Add marinade.

Place in iron pot or ovenproof casserole. Cover and bring to boil. Then reduce heat and simmer 2 to 3 hours.

8 SERVINGS. *3 oz. cooked beef with all ingredients, 83 mg. sodium and 298 calories.*

PINEAPPLE SPARERIBS

Unsalty can do a lot of chewing to earn his 3 ounces.

2 *lbs. spareribs*
2 *cups pineapple chunks*
1 *cup water*
2 *tablespoons cornstarch*
3 *tablespoons wine vinegar*
2 *tablespoons sugar*
¼ *cup pineapple juice*

Fry spareribs, drain on brown paper. Pour off fat and place spareribs and pineapple back into skillet. Simmer 5 minutes. Cook water and cornstarch in double boiler. Stir until thick. Add vinegar and sugar, add pineapple juice. Serve over spareribs.

3 SERVINGS. *17 mg. sodium in recipe excluding spareribs. Cooked spareribs have 80 mg. of sodium in 3 oz. of meat and 250 calories.* You figure this out. Don't count the bones.

There are 594 calories in the sauce. If you need to count your calories watch the amount of sauce you use. What is left over use on cold meat tomorrow.

ROAST LEG OF LAMB

Insert thin slices of garlic under skin on each side, rub with lemon juice. Dredge with flour and season with freshly ground black pepper. Place the meat skin side down in a roasting pan. Serve with Pineapple Sauce.*

3 oz. cooked lamb, 100 mg. sodium and 220 calories.

Pineapple Sauce

¾ cup crushed canned
   pineapple
½ cup pineapple juice
1 cup sugar
¼ teaspoon allspice

¼ teaspoon mustard
¾ cup water
6 drops oil of peppermint
   or 1 teaspoon dried
   mint

Place the pineapple, pineapple juice, sugar, allspice, mustard, and water in a saucepan and cook about 10 minutes over a slow fire until thickened. Cool and add oil of peppermint or dried mint. Chill before serving.

Total sauce, 2 mg. sodium and 980 calories.

BROILED LAMB CHOPS

1. One-inch rib chops weigh about 2 ounces. Loin chops the same thickness weigh about 3 ounces. Rub lamb chops with garlic and lemon juice. Broil 12–14 minutes for medium chops in a 350-degree oven.

2. Dip chops in strong black coffee and rub with ginger. Our Swedish friends always use black coffee to baste their lamb.

The chops also may be rubbed with allspice, basil, dill, ginger, or oregano. Take your choice. They are all wonderful with lamb chops.

3-oz. cooked chop, 100 mg. sodium and 220 calories.

LAMB CHOPS WITH LEMON

4 3-oz. lamb chops
2 lemons
1 large onion
1 green pepper
2 cups canned low-sodium
   tomato juice

¼ teaspoon basil
4 teaspoons unsalted
   butter or margarine

Put meat in skillet. Cover it with thin slices of lemon and onion, slivers of green pepper. Add tomato juice and basil. Dot each chop with butter or margarine. Cover and cook over low heat for 1½ hours. Place on serving platter. The slices of lemon, onion, and green pepper look pretty.

4 SERVINGS. *Per serving, 85 mg. sodium and 248 calories.*

BAKED LAMB CHOPS WITH PINEAPPLE

6 *3-oz. lamb chops*
1 *cup canned crushed pineapple*
1 *teaspoon grated orange rind*

2 *tablespoons finely chopped fresh mint or ½ tablespoon dried mint flakes*
½ *teaspoon dry ginger*
½ *cup pineapple juice*
2 *tablespoons wine vinegar*

Place lamb chops in greased shallow pan. Mix crushed pineapple, orange rind, mint, and ginger and pour over chops. Bake in moderate oven at 350 degrees for 45 to 60 minutes. Then add ½ cup pineapple juice heated with two tablespoons of wine vinegar.

6 SERVINGS. *Per serving, 79 mg. sodium and 209 calories.*

LAMB CHOPS WITH WHITE WINE

6 *3-oz. loin lamb chops*
Garlic bud
Pepper to taste
1 *onion, chopped*
1 *tablespoon parsley, chopped*

2 *tablespoons shallots, chopped*
3 *tablespoons unsalted butter or margarine*
1½ *tablespoons flour*
1 *cup white wine*

Rub chops with garlic and pepper. Brown chops in iron pot or ovenproof dish and keep hot. Sauté onion, parsley, and shallots in butter or margarine. When they are soft, stir in flour and blend well. Add wine and cook until sauce is thickened, stirring constantly. Pour sauce over chops. Cover iron pot with buttered paper and bake in moderate oven for 25 minutes. Remove paper and cook 10 minutes longer in 350-degree oven.

6 SERVINGS. *Per serving, 81 mg. sodium and 254 calories.*

LAMB STEW

A big hand for an old favorite.

3 *lbs. lean lamb, cubed*	1 *tablespoon minced*
3 *tablespoons vegetable*	*fresh parsley*
oil	½ *teaspoon basil*
2 *cups canned low-sodium*	½ *teaspoon thyme*
tomatoes	1 *onion, chopped*
1 *bay leaf*	½ *cup uncooked rice*

Brown meat in oil. Add tomatoes, bay leaf, parsley, basil, and thyme and cook 1½ hours or until tender. Remove fat. Add onion and rice and cook ½ hour.

8 SERVINGS. *3 oz. cooked lamb with all ingredients, 105 mg. sodium and 326 calories.*

CURRIED LAMB AND RICE

Unsalty thinks this is a humdinger.

3 *lbs. lean lamb
    breast, cut in cubes*
3 *tablespoons vegetable
    oil*
Boiling water
2 *small onions, sliced*
1 *tablespoon chopped
    parsley*

1 *bay leaf*
8 *whole black peppers*
⅛ *teaspoon pepper*
⅓ *cup flour*
1½ *teaspoons curry
    powder*
2 *tablespoons cold water*

Brown meat in hot oil, cover with boiling water, add onion, parsley, bay leaf, and peppers. Cover and cook slowly 2 hours or until meat is tender. Strain stock, reserve 2 cups. Mix flour and curry powder, add cold water and blend, stir into stock. Cook until thick. Add meat mixture. Serve on rice.

8 SERVINGS. *3 oz. cooked lamb with all ingredients, 101 mg. sodium and 284 calories (without rice).*

CURRY OF LAMB

This really insured our domestic tranquillity.

1½ *lbs. lean lamb,
    cut in 1-inch cubes*
⅛ *teaspoon pepper*
2 *tablespoons unsalted
    butter or margarine*

1½ *cups hot water*
2 *tablespoons flour*
2 *teaspoons curry powder*
1 *teaspoon sugar*
1 *cup orange juice*

Dredge lamb in flour and pepper. Heat butter or margarine and brown meat. Add water and cook 1½ hours. Combine flour, curry, sugar, mix to smooth paste with orange juice. Add to lamb, stirring constantly. Cook till thickened. Serve with hot Orange Rice.*

6 SERVINGS. *3 oz. cooked lamb with all ingredients, 102 mg. sodium and 290 calories.*

PORK CHOPS

Rub chops with garlic, rosemary, sage, or powdered cloves. Brown chops in a little oil. Reduce heat and cook until well done. Season with pepper. Pork chops may be cooked covered or uncovered. To prevent drying out a small amount of water may be added during the cooking.

3-oz. cooked pork chop, 64 mg. sodium and 280 calories.

PORK CHOPS WITH APPLES AND ORANGES

I seem to be running out of names of my pork-chop recipes.

4 3-oz. pork chops	4 slices onion
1 tablespoon cornstarch	4 slices lemon
2 tablespoons orange juice	¼ teaspoon cinnamon
2 cups pineapple juice	¼ teaspoon cloves
4 slices apple	1 tablespoon brown sugar
4 slices orange	

Brown chops on both sides, pour off drippings. Cook covered over low heat 40 minutes. Stir cornstarch into orange juice until smooth, gradually blend into pineapple juice. Stir constantly until slightly thickened. Simmer a few minutes. Now fine things begin to happen. Top each with slices of apple, orange, onion, and lemon. Sprinkle with cinnamon, cloves, and brown sugar. Bake uncovered at 350 degrees for 25 to 30 minutes.

4 SERVINGS. *Per serving, 54 mg. sodium and 315 calories.*

PORK CHOPS WITH CRANBERRIES

Cloves were discovered by the Dutch on the Moluccas (Spice Islands).

6 3-oz. pork chops	½ teaspoon allspice
4 cups cranberries, ground	½ teaspoon ground
¾ cup strained honey	cloves

Brown chops quickly on both sides in frying pan. Place 3 chops in bottom of greased baking dish. Combine cranberries, honey, allspice, and cloves. Spread half of mixture on first 3 chops, arrange other chops on top and cover with remaining cranberry mixture. Cover and bake for 1 hour at 350 degrees.

6 SERVINGS. *Per serving, 52 mg. sodium and 370 calories.*

PORK CHOPS WITH PARSLEY AND GARLIC

Garlic was also the name of a jig in vogue early in the seventeenth century. The name "twist" does not seem so terrible now, does it?

4 3-oz. pork chops	¼ cup olive oil
½ cup minced parsley	Juice ½ lemon
½ clove garlic	

Mash parsley and garlic to a paste with mortar and pestle (or wooden salad spoon and bowl). Add olive oil and lemon juice. Marinate chops in mixture for 2 hours. Lift chops from marinade. Grill chops in hot skillet until tender. Use marinade for salad greens to be served with chops.

4 SERVINGS. *Per serving, 49 mg. sodium and 338 calories.*

BAKED PORK CHOPS WITH TOMATO

In medieval times the herb sage was thought to prolong life, reduce sorrow and increase wisdom.

6 3-oz. pork chops
2 tablespoons flour
1½ cups sliced onions
⅛ teaspoon pepper
½ teaspoon sage
½ teaspoon rosemary
1 cup water
1 cup canned low-sodium tomatoes
½ teaspoon basil

Flour the chops and pan broil them until slightly browned. Cover with onion, pepper, sage, rosemary, and water. Put on the lid and simmer for ½ hour. Add tomatoes and basil and bake 30 minutes at 400 degrees.

6 SERVINGS. *1 3-oz. uncooked pork chop with all ingredients, 52 mg. sodium and 226 calories.*

PORK CHOPS AND RICE

4 3-oz. pork chops
8 tablespoons uncooked rice
1 cup boiling water
½ teaspoon rosemary
½ teaspoon sage
1 teaspoon sugar
8 slices tomato
½ green pepper, sliced
½ teaspoon basil
Pepper to taste
4 teaspoons unsalted butter or margarine

Brown chops. Place in casserole, put rice around chops. Pour fat off frying pan and add boiling water to frying pan. Add rosemary, sage, and sugar. Pour over chops and rice. Add sliced tomatoes and green pepper. Sprinkle with basil and pepper. Dot with butter or margarine. Cover, bake 45 to 60 minutes at 350 degrees.

4 SERVINGS. *Per serving, 52 mg. sodium and 355 calories.*

ROAST LOIN OF PORK

Now do you believe that an appetizing diet encourages you to stick to your count?

6 lbs. pork loin
Pepper to taste
¼ teaspoon paprika
2 carrots
1 large onion
2 cloves garlic
1 cup water
1 cup dry sauterne

2 whole cloves
Juice of 1 lemon
2 tablespoons currant
  jelly
1 teaspoon dry mustard
2 tablespoons unsalted
  butter or margarine
2 tablespoons flour

Season loin with pepper and paprika and place in roasting pan. Pare carrots, onion, and garlic and cut in small pieces. Place in pan with pork and roast 3½ hours in 350-degree heat.

Remove roast to platter and keep hot. Place roasting pan on top of stove, add water, wine, cloves, lemon juice, jelly, and mustard. Let boil for 20 minutes. Strain sauce, pressing as many vegetables as possible through sieve. Stir in butter or margarine and flour to thicken. Pour over pork.

10 SERVINGS. *3 oz. cooked pork with all ingredients, 77 mg. sodium and 341 calories.*

Roast pork is good basted with:

1 cup burgundy
1 clove garlic

¼ teaspoon rosemary
¼ teaspoon dill

Total recipe, 16 mg. sodium and 390 calories.

Veal may be rubbed with garlic and seasoned with rosemary, savory, or chervil and cooked your favorite way.

VEAL WITH NOODLES

Veal comes from calves that are from 3 to 6 months old and should be cooked thoroughly.

2 lbs. shoulder veal, cubed
Boiling water
6 whole allspice
½ bay leaf
1 clove garlic
½ teaspoon rosemary
1 package Italian
    imported noodles

1½ tablespoons unsalted
    butter or margarine
2 medium onions,
    chopped
½ green pepper, diced
8 medium size mushrooms
2 teaspoons flour
¼ cup cold water

Cover meat with boiling water, add spices, and cook until tender. Remove meat and cut in small pieces. Strain stock, heat to boiling, add noodles, cook until tender. Melt butter or margarine in pan. Sauté onions, pepper, and mushrooms until soft but not brown. Blend in flour, then add cold water and make smooth sauce. Place alternate layers of noodles, meat, and sauce in greased baking dish. Bake 50 to 60 minutes.

6 SERVINGS. *3 oz. cooked veal with all ingredients, 114 mg. sodium and 270 calories.*

½ cup cooked noodles, 3 mg. sodium and 54 calories.

VEAL UCCELLETTI
(Careful Touchable)

1 medium onion, diced
4 tablespoons unsalted
    butter or margarine
6 large mushrooms, sliced
2 4-oz. veal tenderloins
    sliced ⅛ inch thick

¼ teaspoon rosemary
¼ teaspoon sage
1 clove garlic, crushed
Pepper to taste
½ cup dry white wine
Chopped parsley

Sauté (slowly) onion in butter or margarine. Add mushrooms, veal, rosemary, sage, garlic, and pepper. Cook until meat is browned. Add wine, bring to a boil. Remove veal to serving platter. Lessen quantity of wine sauce by boiling wine to a half, then pour over veal. Sprinkle with chopped parsley.

2 SERVINGS. *Per serving, 125 mg. sodium and 492 calories.*

CHILI RICE WITH BEEF

Have this the day that everything went wrong and then one thing will be right.

1 *lb. ground lean beef*
½ *cup chopped onions*
2 *tablespoons olive or vegetable oil*
1½ *cups raw rice*

1½ *cups boiling water*
1¼ *teaspoons chili con carne seasoning powder*
⅛ *teaspoon pepper*

Cook beef with onions in olive or vegetable oil, stirring occasionally. Add rice, boiling water, and seasonings. Cover and simmer 10 to 14 minutes.

4 SERVINGS. *Per serving, 83 mg. sodium and 578 calories.*

STUFFED EGGPLANT CASSEROLE

1 *large eggplant*
1 *cup chopped onions*
1 *cup chopped fresh mushrooms*
1¼ *teaspoons basil or oregano*
½ *teaspoon chervil*
¼ *teaspoon pepper*
2 *tablespoons unsalted butter or margarine*

1 *lb. ground lean beef*
4 *tablespoons canned low-sodium tomato paste*
¼ to ½ *cup low-sodium dry bread crumbs or wheat germ*
1 *tablespoon fresh chopped parsley*

Wash eggplant, wrap it in aluminum foil, and bake 50 minutes. Cut in half, remove pulp to within ½ inch of the outer skin, mash pulp. Sauté onions, mushrooms, and seasonings in the butter or margarine and add to eggplant pulp. Add the meat, tomato paste, and bread crumbs or wheat germ. Mix well and cook until meat is cooked slightly. Spoon mixture into the eggplant shells and place in casserole. Bake 15 to 20 minutes. Garnish with parsley.

4 SERVINGS. *Per serving, 91 mg. sodium and 385 calories.*

KIDNEY BEANS BY GUESS

1 *lb. dried kidney beans*
1 *cup chopped onion*
1 *tablespoon chopped parsley*
1 *teaspoon cumin seed,*[1] *ground*
⅛ *teaspoon fennel seed*
¼ *teaspoon pepper*

1 *cup canned low-sodium tomatoes*
1½ *garlic cloves, minced*
¼ *teaspoon basil*
2 *tablespoons rum*
1 *lb. ground lean beef, sautéed*

---

[1] Cumin is an herb of the parsley family. It is mentioned in the Bible (Matthew 23:23). Look it up. The Mohammedans use it as a condiment.

This is a combination of all my kidney-bean recipes.

Wash beans. Soak overnight. Drain. Put beans in heavy kettle, cover with water, add onion, parsley, cumin, fennel, and pepper. Simmer 1½ hours. Drain if necessary. Put in bean pot with tomatoes, garlic, basil, rum, and sautéed beef. Bake 1 hour in 300-degree oven. This is good served with a little dab of sour cream.

6 SERVINGS. *Per serving, 60 mg. sodium and 462 calories.*

CHILE CON CARNE CASSEROLE

Chile con carne was invented in the United States, not Mexico.

2 *cups kidney beans*	*Pepper to taste*
1 *bay leaf*	1 *tablespoon chili con*
½ *teaspoon cumin*	*carne seasoning powder*
1 *cup onion, chopped*	2½ *cups canned*
2 *cloves garlic, minced*	*low-sodium tomatoes*
2 *tablespoons olive oil*	½ *cup beer*
1 *lb. ground lean beef*	½ *cup low-sodium*
½ *teaspoon oregano*	*cheese*

Cook beans with bay leaf and cumin according to directions on package but *without salt*. Preheat the oven to 375 degrees. Sauté the onion and garlic in the oil for 4 minutes. Add the meat and seasonings and cook until meat is browned. Add the beans, chili powder, and tomatoes and beer. Place the mixture in a large oiled casserole, sprinkle with cheese and bake 30 minutes.

6 SERVINGS. *Per serving, 68 mg. sodium and 655 calories.*

SPANISH OMELETTE

This does seem like a long, long list of ingredients for an omelette. Take time with your meals, and the rewards will gratify not only you but your family and friends.

2 *cups canned dietetic tomatoes*
3 *tablespoons unsalted butter or margarine*
Pepper to taste
Few grains cayenne
¼ *teaspoon thyme*
1 *tablespoon fresh chopped parsley*
1 *bay leaf*
2 *cloves garlic, minced*

1 *tablespoon flour*
½ *cup minced onions*
5 *tablespoons chopped green pepper*
½ *cup white wine*
6 *medium mushrooms sautéed and cut in pieces*
½ *cup cooked fresh peas*
4 *eggs*
1 *tablespoon olive oil*

Combine tomatoes and 1 tablespoon of butter or margarine. Simmer 10 minutes, stirring occasionally. Add pepper and cayenne. Cook 10 minutes. Add thyme, parsley, bay leaf, and garlic. Cook 15 minutes or until sauce is thick. Melt one tablespoon butter or margarine, blend in flour, cook until brown. Add onions, green pepper, brown slightly. Add wine, stirring constantly until slightly thickened. Add mushrooms and peas. Beat eggs until well blended. Add tomato mixture. Heat remaining butter or margarine and olive oil in skillet, pour in egg mixture. Shake skillet until eggs begin to set, lifting edges of omelette to allow uncooked mixture to flow under omelette. When cooked, fold over. Garnish with parsley.

4 SERVINGS. *Per serving, 83 mg. sodium and 278 calories.*

SPAGHETTI SAUCE

The day this was created everyone smiled. At last, to have a low-sodium spaghetti sauce. Serve the regular parmesan cheese to the salties. The Italians spell it parmi-giano.

1 *lb. ground lean beef*
4 *tablespoons olive oil*
1 *chopped onion*
2 *teaspoons minced parsley*
6 *chopped mushrooms*
1 *clove garlic*
½ *teaspoon basil*
1 *bay leaf*

1 *teaspoon sugar*
½ *teaspoon oregano*
¼ *teaspoon allspice*
Pepper to taste
2 *cups canned low-sodium tomatoes*
1 *lb. Italian-import spaghetti*

Fry beef in hot oil until slightly brown. Add onion, parsley, mushrooms, garlic, basil, bay leaf, sugar, oregano, allspice, and pepper. Sauté for 10 minutes. Add tomatoes. Simmer 1 hour. Now—this is a must. Find an Italian store and buy wheat-flour pasta. It cooks tender without salt.

6 SERVINGS. *Per serving (sauce), 61 mg. sodium and 276 calories.*

1 cup cooked pasta, 3 mg. sodium and 192 calories.

21 Fish, Feasts, and Fare

Fresh Fish Calendar

January	Bluefish, Cod, Flounder, Haddock, Mackerel, and Whiting
February	Striped Bass, Cod, Flounder, Haddock, Lake Smelts, and Whiting
March	Striped Bass, Cod, Flounder, Haddock, and Lake Smelts
April	Sea Bass, Cod, Flounder, Haddock, Shad, Salmon, and Lake Smelts
May	Sea Bass, Cod, Haddock, Salmon, and Lake Trout
June	Sea Bass, Bluefish, Butterfish, Haddock, Mackerel (Bonita and Boston), Salmon, Lake Trout, and Tuna
July	Sea Bass, Bluefish, Butterfish, Flounder, Lake Trout, Mackerel (Bonita and Boston), Salmon, Swordfish, and Tuna
August	Sea Bass, Bluefish, Butterfish, Flounder, Lake Trout, Mackerel (Bonita and Boston), Salmon, and Swordfish
September	Sea Bass, Bluefish, Butterfish, Flounder, Lake Trout, Mackerel (Boston), Red Snapper

October	Lake Trout, Red Snapper, Ocean Smelts
November	Cod, Red Snapper, Ocean Smelts, and Whiting
December	Sea Bass, Bluefish, Cod, Flounder, Haddock, Mackerel, Red Snapper, Ocean Smelts, and Whiting

FRESH FLOUNDER IN SHERRY

I shall say this again. Sometimes brine is used in the washing and freezing of fish fillets. Be sure the fillets are cut from fresh whole fish.

1 *lb. flounder fillets, cut into serving pieces*	8 *medium mushrooms chopped fine*
⅓ *cup minced onions*	¼ *cup water*
½ *cup sherry wine*	*Black pepper to taste*

Place fish fillets in shallow greased baking dish. Sprinkle on onion. Add sherry, mushrooms, and water. Season with pepper. Bake in 325-degree oven until fish is tender.

4 SERVINGS. *Per serving, 72 mg. sodium and 124 calories.*

DILL-ICIOUS FILLETS OF FLOUNDER

2 *lbs. fillets of flounder or other white fish*	1 *tablespoon white wine*
1 *cup plain yogurt*	1 *tablespoon lemon juice*
½ *cup low-sodium mayonnaise*	½ *teaspoon each crushed dill and curry powder*

Arrange fillets in shallow oiled baking dish. Mix other

ingredients and pour over all. Bake at 350 degrees for 35 minutes. You may add sautéed mushrooms and white grapes.

6 SERVINGS. *3 oz. cooked flounder with all ingredients, 53 mg. sodium and 146 calories.*

BROILED FRESH HADDOCK WITH LEMON SAUCE

I've read that more haddock is sold than any other fish. When you serve this you will know why.

2 *lbs. fresh haddock*	½ *cup olive or vegetable oil*
3 *tablespoons lemon juice*	½ *teaspoon dry mustard*
Pepper to taste	1½ *teaspoons water*
2 *tablespoons unsalted butter or margarine*	

Preheat the broiler. Cut the fish in serving pieces and place on oiled pan. Brush with one tablespoon of the lemon juice, and season with pepper. Dot with butter or margarine, broil 7 to 10 minutes. While fish is cooking, combine the oil, mustard, water, and remaining lemon juice. Blend well. Heat and pour over fish.

6 SERVINGS. *Per serving, 93 mg. sodium and 319 calories.*

HADDOCK WITH WHITE WINE

2 *lbs. haddock*	½ *cup parsley, chopped*
¼ *cup lemon juice*	3 *tomatoes, peeled and sliced*
Pepper to taste	
½ *cup olive or vegetable oil*	¼ *cup dry white wine, cider or water*
6 *medium onions, sliced*	2 *lemons, sliced*
2 *garlic cloves, sliced*	3 *more tomatoes, sliced*

Sprinkle fish with lemon juice and pepper. Heat oil and add onions, garlic, and parsley. Cook until onions are transparent. Add tomatoes and simmer 5 minutes. Add wine and cook 5 minutes longer. Place half the onion and tomato mixture in greased baking dish. Add fish, and cover with remaining mixture. Arrange lemon slices and the tomato slices over top and bake at 350 degrees until fish flakes—around 30 minutes.

6 SERVINGS. *3 oz. cooked haddock with all ingredients, 80 mg. sodium and 326 calories (with wine).*

BOILED SALMON

This recipe came from our New England states. Happy Fourth of July! Cold salmon is a tradition in New England on Independence Day.

2 *lbs. salmon*	¼ *teaspoon thyme*
2 *tablespoons fresh chopped parsley*	1 *tablespoon vinegar or lemon juice*
1 *bay leaf*	1 *small onion*

Place in pan enough water to cover fish, add other ingredients, and when water boils add the fish. Simmer until tender. Serve with Cucumber Sauce.*

6 SERVINGS. *3 oz. cooked salmon with all ingredients, 91 mg. sodium and 254 calories.*

SAUTEED SALMON STEAKS

2 *lbs. salmon steaks*	2 *tablespoons dry*
¼ *cup unsalted butter or margarine*	*mustard mixed with enough water to make*
¼ *cup apple cider or juice (if not cider season)*	*paste*

FISH, FEASTS, AND FARE

Spread salmon steaks with mustard. Melt butter or margarine in skillet. Add cider or apple juice. Sauté steaks 10 minutes on each side. Cider is excellent in the cooking of any fish.

6 SERVINGS. *3 oz. cooked salmon with all ingredients, 92 mg. sodium and 322 calories.*

BROILED FRESH SALMON STEAKS

The ancient Romans marching across France gave the salmon its name. They named this historic fish *salmo,* the leaper, in admiration for its strength and agility.

4 *salmon steaks*	*Pepper to taste*
4 *tablespoons lime juice*	*4 teaspoons tarragon*
2 *tablespoons unsalted*	*½ cup dry white wine*
butter or margarine	*or dry vermouth*

Place salmon in shallow baking pan. Sprinkle with half the lime juice and dot with butter or margarine. Season with pepper. Sprinkle with half the tarragon and pour wine or vermouth around but not over steaks. Broil for 10 to 15 minutes, basting twice the last 5 minutes. Turn salmon, season with remaining ingredients and broil about 5 minutes longer. Baste twice more. Serve with sauce poured over fish.

4 SERVINGS. *3 oz. cooked salmon with all ingredients, 94 mg. sodium and 325 calories.*

BROILED SWORDFISH

We borrowed this recipe from the Italians, and it is a real favorite of ours. Swordfish should be moist and this surely is. Remember about careful touchables.

Sal is the Latin word for salt, and our word "salary" is

derived from *sal*. You know why? The ancient Roman soldiers were paid in salt instead of money. Hope they weren't unsalties.

2 *lbs. swordfish (fresh or frozen)*	¼ *cup olive oil*
Juice of two lemons	2 *teaspoons oregano*
1 *teaspoon fresh mint or*	*Pepper to taste*
½ teaspoon dried mint chopped	

Blend well lemon juice, mint, oil, oregano, and pepper. Brush fish with mixture. Place on preheated broiler rack about 4 inches below flame. Broil 5 minutes or until slightly brown, turn, brush again with mixture. Broil about 7 minutes or until done. Brush again with mixture before serving. Serve hot.

6 SERVINGS. *3 oz. cooked swordfish with all ingredients, 91 mg. sodium and 229 calories.*

BAKED OYSTERS

Sometimes our unsalty has a craving for the taboo shellfish. (This may be indulged if your doctor says so.) The oyster comes to the rescue, but watch out for the number you serve. Each oyster has approximately 10 mg. sodium. So let's try baked oysters with a sauce. Taking the scientific route you could use 5 oysters per serving, which keeps the sodium content well within the allowed serving of a piece of meat. It does cheer our dieter, and that can be good medicine too.

For each serving (the old salt can have a dozen if he wants):

5 *oysters*	1 *teaspoon chopped parsley*
4 *teaspoons unsalted butter or margarine*	*Freshly ground black pepper to taste*

Remove oysters from shells and drain them. Place each oyster back on the half shell with a small piece of unsalted butter or margarine on top. Place in baking pan, sprinkle with parsley and pepper, bake in 400-degree oven for 6 to 8 minutes.

1 SERVING. *Total recipe, 52 mg. sodium and 225 calories.*

Sauce

2 *tablespoons unsalted butter or margarine*
Juice of 1 lemon
Juice of ½ onion

¼ *teaspoon tarragon vinegar*
⅛ *teaspoon dry mustard*

Melt the butter, stir in the other ingredients, and pour over oysters. Serve hot.

1 SERVING. *Total recipe, 7 mg. sodium and 229 calories.*

COCKTAIL OYSTERS

1 *pint oysters*
1 *pint oyster liquor*
½ *tablespoon whole black pepper*
½ *tablespoon allspice*

½ *lemon, cut in thin slices*
Vinegar and cayenne to taste

Place oysters and liquor in top of double boiler. Heat enough to curl edges, drain. Keep liquor. Dry oysters with paper towels. Boil liquor with spices about 30 minutes. Pour over oysters and lemon. Add vinegar and cayenne. Let stand in refrigerator for 24 hours. Will keep for days.

There are about 2 dozen oysters in one pint, depending on size of oyster.

10 mg. sodium in 1 oyster and 20 calories.

OYSTER COCKTAIL

5 *oysters in half shell.*

Serve with 2 tablespoons low-sodium chili sauce with bit of cayenne and lemon juice and 1 tablespoon of low-sodium mayonnaise, or 1 tablespoon sherry mixed with a bit of cayenne. Grated fresh horseradish or lemon juice may be added.
1 SERVING.
Each oyster, 10 mg. sodium and 20 calories.
1 tablespoon low-sodium chili sauce, 0.7 mg. sodium and 17 calories.
1 tablespoon low-sodium mayonnaise, 6 mg. sodium and 92 calories.
1 tablespoon sherry, 2.3 mg. sodium and 22 calories.

UNSALTY'S OYSTER "STEW"

5 *oysters*	*Few grains cayenne*
1 *tablespoon unsalted butter or margarine*	¼ *teaspoon paprika*
	¼ *cup oyster liquor*
1 *tablespoon low-sodium chili sauce*	2 *tablespoons cream*
	1 *piece low-sodium toast*
½ *teaspoon lemon juice*	

Place oysters, butter or mayonnaise, chili sauce, lemon juice, cayenne, paprika, oyster liquor in a deep pan. Cook about 1 minute, stirring constantly. Add cream, and when mixture comes to a boiling point, pour over toast placed in a soup plate. You may add grated fresh horseradish, if you wish.
1 SERVING. *Total recipe, 68 mg. sodium and 390 calories.*

SCALLOPED OYSTERS

5 *oysters (for each
  serving)*
6 *tablespoons low-sodium
  bread crumbs mixed
  with 1 teaspoon chives
  and few grains cayenne
  pepper*

1 *tablespoon unsalted
  butter or margarine*
Oyster liquid
1 *tablespoon cream*

Place 3 tablespoons of the bread-crumb mixture in bottom of individual oiled baking dish. Place oysters on this mixture, add rest of bread-crumb mixture on top of each oyster, and dot with butter or margarine. Fill dishes with oyster liquid mixed with cream. Bake in a 350-degree oven for 6 to 8 minutes.

1 SERVING. *Per serving, 60 mg. sodium and 324 calories.*

22   Poultry, Plumage, and Prey

ROAST CHICKEN

1 *4-lb. roasting chicken*
3 *tablespoons unsalted*
  butter or margarine

1 *tablespoon lemon juice*
Piece of lemon peel

Have chicken at room temperature. Rub chicken with butter or margarine and lemon juice. Place 1 tablespoon of butter or margarine and lemon peel inside the chicken. Roast chicken uncovered in 300-degree oven until tender, basting often. Chicken requires 30 to 35 minutes per pound. Instead of lemon peel and butter, a piece of low-sodium bread fried in unsalted butter or margarine and rubbed with garlic may be substituted.

6 SERVINGS. *3 oz. cooked chicken breast with butter or margarine and lemon juice (approximately), 90 mg. sodium and 211 calories.*

OVEN-BAKED SPRING BROILER

A real standby. This, with new potatoes served with nutmeg and unsalted butter or margarine and fresh peas with added mint jelly, makes you feel as you should on a lush spring day.

Rub small broiler with unsalted butter or margarine. Place in pan with 2 tablespoons of water. Place slice of onion and a pinch of rosemary on each half. Bake in 400-degree oven for 35 minutes. Baste chicken every 10 minutes. We sometimes like to top it off with a few sprinkles of sherry.

4 SERVINGS.

3 oz. cooked chicken breast, 89 mg. sodium and 186 calories.

3 oz. cooked chicken leg, 124 mg. sodium and 196 calories.

BROILED CHICKEN

A good after-bridge-club dish.

1 2-lb. broiler, quartered
1 garlic bud
Pepper to taste
½ teaspoon tarragon

1 cup hot water
2 tablespoons unsalted
   butter or margarine

Rub chicken with garlic. Brown quickly on both sides under hot broiler. Place chicken in baking dish and season with pepper and tarragon. Bake in 350-degree oven and baste with hot water and butter until tender.

4 SERVINGS. *3 oz. cooked chicken breast with all ingredients, 90 mg. sodium and 236 calories.*

CHICKEN WITH ALMOND RICE

When and if you go to Palestine, plan your trip for January. The almond trees are in bloom, and the whole land a breathtaking sight. The almond is the kernel of the fruit of these beautiful trees, which resembles a peach.

2 whole chicken breasts (split)

6 tablespoons vegetable oil

2 tablespoons minced onion

8 mushrooms, sliced

1 teaspoon lemon juice

1½ low-sodium chicken flavored bouillon cubes mixed with 1½ cups water

Pepper to taste

¾ cup uncooked rice

⅓ cup slivered blanched unsalted almonds

Preheat the oven to 300 degrees. Brown chicken breasts in oil. Remove and drain on paper towel. Sauté onion in oil remaining in pan. Add mushrooms and lemon juice and sauté 3 minutes longer. Add chicken-bouillon mixture, pepper, and rice. Bring to a boil and simmer 3 minutes more. Stir in almonds. Place rice mixture in oiled casserole. Top with chicken. Cover and bake 45 minutes. Watch the calories in this recipe.

4 SERVINGS. *3 oz. cooked chicken with all ingredients, 97 mg. sodium and 599 calories.*

HERB CHICKEN

Unsalty will take a shine to this. So will salty.

1 chicken 3–3½ lbs. cut in pieces

1 teaspoon marjoram

1 teaspoon thyme

1 tablespoon chopped parsley

Freshly ground black pepper

4 tablespoons unsalted butter or margarine

Wash and dry chicken. Place in greased low baking dish, and sprinkle with marjoram and thyme. Let stand 1 hour. Sprinkle with parsley and pepper. Dot with margarine or butter. Bake in 400-degree oven for 35 to 45 minutes or until tender. Give unsalty the breast meat. For company, heat pineapple chunks and place under chicken.

4 SERVINGS.

3 oz. cooked chicken breast with all ingredients, 90 mg. sodium and 236 calories.

3 oz. cooked chicken leg with all ingredients, 125 mg. sodium and 246 calories.

CHICKEN CACCIATORE

Our guests never miss the salt in this wonderful chicken. Ask friends who like a little garlic. In Italian, *cacciatore* means hunter or sportsman, and they know about good food. Garlic skin will come off easily if hot water is poured over the garlic bud.

3 *whole chicken breasts (split)*	¼ *teaspoon rosemary*
¼ *cup olive oil*	¼ *teaspoon basil*
1 *onion, chopped fine*	4 *fresh tomatoes cut in small pieces or 2 cups canned low-sodium tomatoes*
2 *tablespoons chopped green pepper*	
½ *cup dry white wine*	1 *bud garlic, minced*
1 *bay leaf*	*Pepper to taste*

Cook chicken in olive oil for about 20 minutes or until brown. Remove to platter, then add onion and green pepper and cook until transparent. Stir in wine and add remaining ingredients and cook for about 15 minutes or until tender.

6 SERVINGS. *3 oz. cooked chicken with all ingredients, 95 mg. sodium and 308 calories.*

CHICKEN CREOLE

1 *3-lb. frying chicken*   1 *tablespoon fresh minced*
   (cut in pieces)   *parsley*
¼ *cup olive oil*   1 *bay leaf*
4 *cups canned*   3 *cloves garlic, minced*
   low-sodium tomatoes   ¼ *teaspoon basil*
2 *tablespoons unsalted*   1 *tablespoon flour*
   butter or margarine   ½ *cup minced onion*
⅛ *teaspoon pepper*   5 *tablespoons chopped*
Few grains cayenne   *green pepper*
¼ *teaspoon thyme*   ½ *cup red wine*

Wash and dry chicken. Sauté in olive oil. Brown on both sides. In another pan combine tomatoes and 1 tablespoon of butter or margarine. Simmer 10 minutes, stirring occasionally. Add pepper, cayenne, thyme, parsley, bay leaf, garlic, and basil. Cook 15 minutes or until sauce is thick. Melt 1 tablespoon butter or margarine, blend in flour, cook until brown. Add onions and green pepper. Brown slightly, add wine, stirring constantly until slightly thickened. Add chicken, cover, simmer 45 minutes.

6 SERVINGS. *3 oz. cooked chicken breast with all ingredients, 102 mg. sodium and 361 calories.*

CHICKEN MARENGO

Marengo is the name of a village in Italy where Napoleon defeated the Austrians on June 14, 1800. Maybe this recipe is why Napoleon said, "An army travels on its stomach." June 14 also celebrates an important day for America—Flag Day.

1 4-lb. frying chicken cut up in serving pieces	¼ teaspoon thyme
	2 tablespoons chopped parsley
4 tablespoons olive oil or vegetable oil	1 tablespoon canned low-sodium tomato paste (or fresh tomato may be used)
2 tablespoons flour	
½ cup water	
½ cup dry white wine	8 large mushrooms
1 clove garlic, minced	Pepper to taste
Small bay leaf	

Fry chicken in oil in deep pan. Turn frequently so it is evenly brown and crisp. Remove chicken. Stir flour in drippings. Add water and wine, blend well. Add garlic, spices, tomato paste, and mushrooms. Season with pepper. Replace chicken in sauce, cover pan, and simmer 1 hour.

In place of wine, water, and tomato paste, 2 cups of canned low-sodium tomatoes may be used.

6 SERVINGS. *3 oz. cooked chicken breast with all ingredients, 94 mg. sodium and 298 calories.*

CHICKEN IN SOUR CREAM WITH PAPRIKA

In 1937, Professor Albert von Szent-Györgyi, a Hungarian scientist, discovered Vitamin C in paprika and won the Nobel Prize for his research.

This is good enough for your most elegant guest.

1 2½-lb. frying chicken cut into serving pieces	¼ cup finely chopped onion
¼ cup olive oil	¼ teaspoon thyme
½ cup flour	2 teaspoons paprika
½ teaspoon pepper	4 tablespoons sour cream

Wash and dry chicken. Heat oil in a skillet. Mix flour and pepper. Dredge chicken. Fry the chicken in the oil until brown. Remove and drain. Sauté the onion in the oil until tender. Return chicken to pan and sprinkle with thyme. Cover and cook gently 30 minutes until done. Sprinkle the chicken with paprika. Stir in sour cream.

4 SERVINGS. *3 oz. cooked chicken breast with all ingredients, 96 mg. sodium and 412 calories.*

TARRAGON CHICKEN I

1 *3-lb. frying chicken*	2 *tablespoons brandy*
3 *tablespoons flour*	½ *cup white wine*
Pepper to taste	1 *teaspoon tarragon*
¼ *cup unsalted butter or margarine*	12 *small onions*
	8 *mushrooms*

Dredge chicken in flour. Season with pepper. Melt 2 tablespoons of the butter or margarine in heavy skillet and brown chicken lightly. Heat brandy, then light and pour over chicken. Add wine, tarragon, onions, and mushrooms. Cover and cook slowly 40–45 minutes. Melt remaining butter or margarine. Pour over chicken and serve.

4 SERVINGS. *3 oz. cooked chicken breast, 97 mg. sodium and 298 calories.*

TARRAGON CHICKEN II

The herb tarragon has a variety of uses. Try just a few sprinkles on a green salad.

3 *whole chicken breasts, split*	5 *tablespoons unsalted butter or margarine*
1 *onion sliced thin*	3 *tablespoons flour*
1 *carrot sliced thin*	*Pepper to taste*
½ *teaspoon tarragon*	1 *egg yolk, slightly beaten*
½ *cup dry white wine*	3 *tablespoons heavy cream*
Boiling water	

Pull skin off chicken breasts. Place chicken, onion, carrot, tarragon, and wine in a large saucepan. Add enough boiling water to cover chicken. Cover, simmer about 25 minutes or until tender. Remove chicken and keep warm. Strain liquid. Boil gently until liquid is reduced to 2 cups, about 1 hour. Then melt the 3 tablespoons of butter or margarine. Stir in flour and pepper. Gradually add the 2 cups of chicken broth. Cook, stirring constantly, until mixture is smooth and thickened. Add the 2 tablespoons butter and simmer gently 5 minutes, stirring occasionally. Combine egg yolk and cream. Stir into hot sauce. Serve over chicken breasts.

6 SERVINGS. *3 oz. cooked chicken with all ingredients, 104 mg. sodium and 339 calories.*

CURRIED TURKEY

This is an unusually good dish for leftover turkey. Use the white meat because the sodium content is less than the dark. Serve with rice cooked with orange juice.

3 *tablespoons unsalted butter or margarine*
2 *cups turkey (cooked and cubed)*
1 *can pineapple chunks (drained)*
1 *teaspoon curry powder*
2½ *tablespoons flour*

¾ *cup milk and ¾ cup low-sodium milk (mixed)*
2 *teaspoons lemon juice*
2 *ripe halved avocados (dipped in lemon juice)*

Melt butter in a flat saucepan and add turkey and pineapple. Sprinkle mixture with curry powder, flour, and milk. Cook 5 minutes, stirring constantly. Add lemon juice. Fill avocado halves with mixture. Bake 30 minutes at 350 degrees to 375 degrees. Garnish with peach or apricot. Watch the calories!

4 SERVINGS. *Per serving, 76 mg. sodium and 678 calories.*

ROAST TURKEY

Bake your favorite way, but use unsalted vegetable oil to brush the legs, breast, and wings.

CASSEROLE OF DUCK

1 5-lb. duck (cut up)
2 tablespoons flour
3 tablespoons vegetable oil
Pepper to taste
1 medium onion, chopped fine

3 tablespoons chopped fresh parsley
⅛ teaspoon rosemary
1 teaspoon thyme
Clove of garlic
1 cup red wine

Dredge the duck with flour and sear well in oil. Remove pieces to a casserole and season with pepper. Add onion, parsley, rosemary, thyme, and garlic. Pour wine over duck. Cover casserole. Place in 350-degree oven and cook 2 hours.

6 SERVINGS. *3 oz. cooked duck breast with all ingredients, 83 mg. sodium and 305 calories.*

ROAST DUCKLING

Ducks became Long Island ducks in 1873 when they arrived on ships from China. They still speak with a Chinese accent, I think.

1 5-lb. Long Island duckling
1 clove garlic
4 carrots

8 medium onions
1 orange
3 tablespoons currant jelly

Rub duckling with garlic. Place in uncovered pan and bake 20–30 minutes per pound in 350-degree oven, basting every 10 minutes. Remove duckling to heated pan. Skim off excess fat from duck juices. Reduce juices over high heat to one fourth the original quantity. Slice carrots and onions and cook in gravy. Cut orange rind in strips, boil in a little water a few minutes. Set aside. Squeeze the juice of an orange in the duck gravy. Add currant jelly, mixing well. Decorate duck with orange rind and serve with carrots and onions.

6 SERVINGS.
3 oz. cooked duck breast with all ingredients, 116 mg. sodium and 286 calories.
Without carrots, 89 mg. sodium and 273 calories.

FRENCH RABBIT

If you like rabbit it is lower in sodium than most meats. I don't. I always think about the poor little bunny that romps in our garden.

1 *5-lb. rabbit cut in 8–10 pieces*
2 *tablespoons vegetable oil*
2 *onions cut small*
1 *bay leaf*
Pepper to taste
1 *tablespoon flour*
1 *cup warm water*
½ *cup red wine*

Fry rabbit in vegetable oil. Transfer to saucepan. Brown onions in same skillet, add to rabbit with bay leaf and pepper. Sprinkle with flour and mix. Add water, wine. Cover, bring to boil. Turn heat low, simmer 1½ hours. Add more water if necessary.

6 SERVINGS. *3 oz. cooked rabbit with all ingredients, 58 mg. sodium and 209 calories.*

23 Vegetables, Vitamins, and Vitality

Why didn't someone ever tell me that vegetables lost some of their vitamins if you added salt while they were cooking? I read it the other day in small print. That's quite important to the health of our nation and should be headlined somewhere. Why doesn't some editor print that on the front page? The weather forecast is printed every day on the front page, and it isn't always right, but not to salt your vegetables while cooking because it drains out some of the vitamins is always right. Salty should salt afterward, for his own good.

Lovely fresh vegetables are so much tastier than ones that come in packages or cans. I am so worried that the next generation will just open packages and cans and call out, "Dinner is served." They will probably have some new chemical by then that will heat the cans and packages when in contact with a certain type of a china plate. Good for those who hate cooking and housework.

In fact, I was so concerned about this that I did something about it. Susan had been exposed to "higher education," and I wondered how much good this "higher education" would do her when it came to preparing good, nourishing meals in her own home someday. So, one summer, home she stayed. There was no summer job. By the end of the summer she was an experienced, creative cook. She tried dishes I never dared to try, and they were delicious. She taught me many tricks to flavor her dad's low-sodium diet. The books she read were not on her college reading list—whole cookbooks would be read at one sitting. The tenderness and sweetness of a fresh vegetable bought an hour before dinner at a farmer's stand taught her something. She learned, too, about budgets. At first we didn't eat too well the last two days of the week. That improved with time, as did the state of the kitchen sink and floor.

ASPARAGUS

I cook asparagus in the bottom of a double boiler with ½ cup of boiling water in the bottom. Put the top of the boiler upside down like a hat and cook 12 to 15 minutes.

Cooked asparagus is tasty served with a little lemon juice, or you may add ¼ teaspoon dry mustard or ¼ teaspoon thyme to the water the last 5 minutes of cooking.
6 stalks have 2.0 mg. sodium and 22 calories.

For a simple sauce you may heat low-sodium mayonnaise mixed with a small amount of lemon juice. You might like a little white wine mixed with melted unsalted butter or margarine with a sprinkle of sesame seeds.

ASPARAGUS WITH MARJORAM

2 *lbs. asparagus*
4 *tablespoons unsalted*
   butter or margarine
Pepper to taste

¼ *teaspoon marjoram*
1 *tablespoon fresh*
   parsley, minced
Juice of 1 lemon

Cook asparagus your way or mine (see above).

Mix butter or margarine with pepper, marjoram, parsley, and lemon juice. Pour on asparagus.

6 SERVINGS. *Per serving, 3 mg. sodium and 89 calories.*

STRING BEANS

Allow 1 lb. for 4 servings and 1¼ cups of water. (1 lb. equals 3 cups cut beans) Cook beans in boiling water for about 20 minutes.

½ cup, 1 mg. sodium and 23 calories.

Green beans are good with these combinations of herbs. Add last five minutes of cooking time:

1. ½ teaspoon dill
   (ground or seed)
   ¼ teaspoon rosemary
2. ½ teaspoon dry
   mustard
   ½ teaspoon caraway
   seed
3. ¼ teaspoon savory
   ¼ teaspoon mustard
4. 2 tablespoons mint
   jelly (pure—without
   added preservatives)

A dash of olive oil, vinegar, garlic powder, sugar, or minced onion may be added, and always a little unsalted butter or margarine.

4 SERVINGS.

STRING BEANS DELUXE

1 lb. string beans
½ cup hot water
2 tablespoons olive or
  vegetable oil
1 small onion, chopped
1 clove garlic, minced
1 large tomato, chopped
1 tablespoon white wine

1 tablespoon green
  pepper, chopped
1 tablespoon parsley,
  minced
½ teaspoon marjoram
⅛ teaspoon cinnamon or
  allspice

Cut string beans in half. Place in saucepan. Add hot water. Cover and cook 20 to 30 minutes over low flame.

In separate pan heat *oil*. Add onion and garlic to oil. Cook slowly 10 minutes. Peel tomato and cut into oil and onion mixture. Add wine, pepper, herbs, and spices. Simmer 10 minutes, add beans, stir, cover, and cook 10 minutes more.

4 SERVINGS. *Per serving, 6 mg. sodium and 125 calories.*

STRING BEANS WITH MINT JELLY

1 *lb. string beans*	1 *tablespoon unsalted*
3 *tablespoons vinegar*	*margarine or butter*
1 *tablespoon mint jelly*[1]	¼ *teaspoon rosemary*
(pure)	

Cut beans (julienne). Cook covered 20 to 25 minutes in rapidly boiling water. Add vinegar, jelly, butter or margarine, and rosemary. Mix well.

4 SERVINGS. *Per serving, 3 mg. sodium and 74 calories.*

MINTED STRING BEANS

The mint family has over 25 species, and all are used for flavorings and medicines. The most common are spearmint and peppermint. The herb mint is mentioned in the Bible.

1 *lb. string beans*	1½ *tablespoons unsalted*
¼ *cup sugar*	*butter or margarine*
Hot bean liquor	½ *tablespoon flour*
1 *tablespoon vinegar*	1 *teaspoon dried mint*

Wash beans. Cut (julienne). Cook covered in a small amount of boiling water until just tender—20 to 25 minutes. Save liquor.

---

[1] If pure mint jelly isn't available, mix pure apple jelly with a little mint sauce.

SAUCE

Put sugar in heavy frying pan and stir over low heat until melted. Add bean liquor and vinegar and cook until sugar is dissolved. Melt butter or margarine, blend in flour and mint and add hot liquid, slowly, stirring constantly, and cook until thickened. Pour over beans.

4 SERVINGS. *Per serving, 2 mg. sodium and 121 calories.*

SWEET-SOUR GREEN BEANS

1 *package frozen green beans or 1 lb. fresh beans*
2 *tablespoons unsalted butter or margarine*
2 *tablespoons finely chopped onion*

1 *tablespoon vinegar*
½ *teaspoon sugar*
¼ *teaspoon curry powder*
Pepper to taste

Cook beans according to directions on package but without salt, or cook fresh beans until tender. Melt butter or margarine, add onion, and cook until tender but not brown. Stir in vinegar, sugar, curry, and pepper. Pour over hot cooked and drained beans.

4 SERVINGS. *Per serving, 2 mg. sodium and 63 calories.*

BROCCOLI

You should soak broccoli in cold water for 10 to 15 minutes. Shake off water and remove large leaves and tough part of the stalks. Gash bottoms of stalks. Cook broccoli in 1 inch boiling water in covered pan for 10 to 12 minutes.

½ cup broccoli, 11 mg. sodium and 22 calories.

Combination of herbs are for 4 servings. Add last 5 minutes of cooking time:

1. ¼ *teaspoon nutmeg*
   ¼ *teaspoon dry mustard*

2. ¼ *teaspoon caraway seed*
   ¼ *teaspoon basil*

3. ¼ *teaspoon curry powder*
   ¼ *teaspoon oregano*

4. ¼ *teaspoon dill (ground or seed)*
   ¼ *teaspoon dry mustard*

5. ¼ *teaspoon chervil*
   1 *garlic bud*

Heated unsalted butter or margarine or low-sodium mayonnaise mixed with lemon juice may be used as a sauce. Garnish with paprika.

4 SERVINGS.

BROCCOLI WITH LEMON

1 *lb. broccoli*
2 *teaspoons sugar*
½ *teaspoon paprika*
½ *teaspoon dried mustard*

2 *tablespoons lemon juice*
2 *tablespoons unsalted butter or margarine*

Trim, split, and wash broccoli stalks. Cook in a little boiling water about 10 minutes. Blend sugar, paprika, and mustard. Add lemon juice, melted butter, or margarine. Mix well and pour over broccoli.

4 SERVINGS. *Per serving, 10 mg. sodium and 89 calories.*

BRUSSELS SPROUTS

Pull off wilted leaves, soak sprouts 10 minutes in cold water, drain. Gash stem, drop in boiling water. Reduce heat and simmer 10 minutes.

There are 15 sprouts in a frozen package and 18 in a pound in the fresh-vegetable department. Allow 4 to 5 per serving.

9 medium, 11 mg. sodium and 60 calories.

Add last 5 minutes of cooking time:

1. ¼ *teaspoon dill*
     (ground or seed)
   ¼ *teaspoon dry*
     mustard

2. ¼ *teaspoon nutmeg*
   ¼ *teaspoon caraway*
     seed

3. ¼ *teaspoon basil*
   ¼ *teaspoon dry*
     mustard

Brussels sprouts may be topped with unsalted butter or margarine with a dash of lemon juice or vinegar. For a wonderful topping, mix nutmeg with sour cream.

4 SERVINGS.

CASSEROLE OF BRUSSELS SPROUTS

These are better than salty's sprouts.

1½ *tablespoons*
  unsalted butter or
  margarine
¼ *cup chopped onion*
1½ *tablespoons flour*
Pepper to taste
1 *teaspoon basil*

½ *teaspoon dry mustard*
1 *cup cooked fresh*
  tomatoes (peeled) or
  canned low-sodium
  tomatoes
1½ *cups Brussels sprouts*

Heat butter or margarine, add onion, and cook slowly until yellow. Blend in flour, pepper, basil, mustard, and add tomatoes. Stir and cook until mixture is thick. Put the sprouts into oiled baking dish and add mixture. Bake at 350-degree heat about 30 minutes.

4 SERVINGS. *Per serving, 9 mg. sodium and 83 calories.*

CABBAGE

Place cabbage in boiling water in covered pan, allow to simmer for 7 to 10 minutes.

1 cup cabbage shredded, 12.8 mg. sodium and 20 calories.

These herb combinations can be used:

1. ¼ *teaspoon fennel*
   ¼ *teaspoon nutmeg*

2. ¼ *teaspoon oregano*
   ¼ *teaspoon dry mustard*

3. ¼ *teaspoon caraway seed*
   ¼ *teaspoon dill (ground or seed)*

4. ¼ *teaspoon savory*
   ¼ *teaspoon cumin seed or tarragon*

Cabbage may be topped with unsalted butter or margarine. If you can stand the calories or sodium count and your doctor approves, a little sour cream is very good. You know vinegar and lemon juice and cabbage go steady too. Garnish with parsley.

4 SERVINGS.

RED CABBAGE

This recipe was awarded a prize by the London *Daily Express* on Christmas 1927.

1 *red cabbage*
1 *tablespoon unsalted butter or margarine*
Pepper to taste
½ *teaspoon nutmeg*
1 *tablespoon sugar*
1 *medium onion, chopped*

2 *cups hot water*
2 *apples, sliced*
4 *whole cloves*
1 *tablespoon vinegar*
2 *tablespoons raspberry or currant jelly*

Slice cabbage and soak in cold water. Heat butter or margarine in saucepan. Add cabbage, pepper, nutmeg, sugar, and onion. Simmer for about 20 minutes. Then add hot water, apples, cloves, and vinegar. Cover and cook slowly until tender. The final touch is topping of currant or raspberry jelly.

8 SERVINGS. *Per serving, 10 mg. sodium and 69 calories.*

SWEET-SOUR RED CABBAGE

2 *cups red cabbage*
½ *teaspoon cornstarch*
2 *teaspoons water*

⅛ *cup vinegar*
3 *tablespoons sugar*
¼ *teaspoon tarragon*

Shred cabbage coarsely. Cover in boiling water and cook 7 to 10 minutes. Drain all but ½ cup water. Add cornstarch mixed with 2 teaspoons of water, vinegar, sugar, and tarragon. Cook a few minutes.

4 SERVINGS. *Per serving, 7 mg. sodium and 48 calories.*

CARROTS

Carrots are not always allowed on sodium-restricted diets. Go by the list your doctor gave you. They are used in this book because it is a family cookbook, and carrots are important for the salties.

Peel or don't peel the carrots. Cook in small amount of boiling water covered for 20 to 30 minutes. Shredded carrots need less cooking. Somehow carrots are easy for me to burn. Watch them better than I do.

½ cup, 32 mg. of sodium and 25 calories. Watch your count.

After 10 minutes of cooking time add any of the following combinations:

1. ½ *teaspoon sugar*
   ½ *teaspoon cinnamon*

2. ½ *teaspoon mint*
   ½ *teaspoon marjoram*

3. 1 *bay leaf*
   ¼ *teaspoon thyme or dill (ground or seed)*

4. 1 *tablespoon mint jelly (pure—without added preservatives)*

5. ¼ *teaspoon curry*
   ¼ *teaspoon ginger*

6. 1 *tablespoon honey*
   ¼ *teaspoon allspice*

Parsley may always be added. Lemon juice, too, plus unsalted butter or margarine. Season with pepper.
4 SERVINGS.

CAULIFLOWER

Most cookbooks tell you to soak cauliflower head down in salted water for 15 minutes. DON'T YOU DARE! But do this. Soak it head down in cold water or break the whole thing up in pieces and just soak. Gash the stalks. Cook cauliflower head up this time in boiling water. Simmer uncovered for 12 to 14 minutes.

½ cup, 18 mg. sodium and 15 calories.

Add juice of ½ lemon to boiling water. Then these combinations you add last 5 minutes of cooking time:

1. ¼ teaspoon nutmeg
   or mace
   2 teaspoons chopped
   parsley

2. ¼ teaspoon rosemary
   ¼ teaspoon dill
   (ground or seed)
   2 teaspoons chopped
   parsley

3. ¼ teaspoon tarragon
   2 teaspoons chopped
   parsley

Always pepper to taste and add melted unsalted butter or margarine.
4 SERVINGS.

BAKED CORN ON COB

This is quite an invention for unsalty's corn.
Remove husks and silk from fresh corn. Mix peanut butter and butter or margarine. Spread on corn. Wrap loosely in foil and bake for 20 to 25 minutes.
1 ear of corn, 3 mg. sodium and 85 calories.
1 teaspoon low-sodium peanut butter, 2.5 mg. sodium and 34 calories.
1 teaspoon unsalted butter or margarine, 0.5 mg. sodium and 34 calories.

CORN ON COB

Drop fresh hulled corn in 1 inch of boiling water. Add 1 tablespoon of sugar. Cover the kettle and boil 5 to 10 minutes. Spread with unsalted butter or margarine and sprinkle with garlic or onion powder.

CORN CURRY

Have this at your next barbecue.

3 *tablespoons unsalted butter or margarine*
1½ *cups fresh or frozen corn*
2 *tablespoons chopped green pepper*
2 *tablespoons chopped onion*
½ *teaspoon curry powder*
4 *tablespoons dairy sour cream*
Pepper to taste

Melt butter or margarine in skillet. Add vegetables and curry. Cover. Cook over low heat until vegetables are just tender, 8 to 10 minutes. Stir in sour cream, season with pepper. Reheat, stirring constantly.

4 SERVINGS. *Per serving, 9 mg. sodium and 178 calories.*

LIMA BEANS

Cook Lima beans in an inch of boiling water, covered. Simmer for 20 minutes. (1 pint serves 4.) After 10 minutes of cooking time add ¼ teaspoon sage. When tender, add 2 tablespoons unsalted butter or margarine, 3 teaspoons lemon juice, and 1 tablespoon chopped parsley or 2 teaspoons chives and ground black pepper. If permitted a little sour cream is divine.

Fresh stewed tomatoes, onions, or sautéed mushrooms may be added.

4 SERVINGS. *½ cup Lima beans (remember fresh only), 1 mg. sodium and 100 calories.*

MUSHROOMS

1 lb. serves 4.
Wipe mushrooms with damp cloth or wash and dry them. Slice them if you want. Sauté mushrooms in 2 tablespoons of unsalted butter or margarine for each pound.

You may add any of the following combinations:

1. ¼ *teaspoon ginger*
   ¼ *teaspoon rosemary or marjoram*
   ⅛ *teaspoon black pepper*
   ½ *teaspoon lemon juice*

2. ¼ *teaspoon paprika*
   ¼ *teaspoon basil*

   ½ *teaspoon lemon juice*
   ⅛ *teaspoon black pepper*

3. ¼ *teaspoon tarragon*
   ¼ *teaspoon paprika*
   ⅛ *teaspoon black pepper*
   ½ *teaspoon lemon juice*

4 SERVINGS. *8 large mushrooms, 10 mg. sodium and 25 calories.*

MUSHROOMS AMHERST

As long as these mushrooms were named for Amherst, I should tell you that Yale was founded on spice money. Elihu Yale became wealthy on his spice business in India and was able to establish Yale University on his fortune.

20 *medium-sized mushroom caps*
⅛ *lb. unsalted butter or margarine*
Powdered garlic
Powdered onion
Marjoram

½ *pint sour cream*
3 *tablespoons finely chopped parsley*
6 *small finely chopped green onions, tops and bottoms*
Pepper to taste

Sauté the mushroom caps in the butter or margarine slowly, so that the mushroom juice combines with the butter or margarine. Sprinkle liberally with powdered garlic, onion, marjoram, and pepper. Sprinkle them again when you turn them. In the meantime, combine the sour cream, parsley, and onions. When the mushrooms are brown and tender (15 to 20 minutes) take the pan off the fire and add ½ of the sour-cream mixture. With a spatula, scrape the brown butter and mushroom juice from the bottom of the pan and stir it in with the sour cream until you have a smooth, golden sauce. Serve immediately. Use the other half of the sour-cream mixture on baked potatoes.

Use as a side dish on rice, potatoes, or meat, or on a slice of low-sodium bread for a luncheon dish.

Mushrooms are fairly high in protein as compared to many vegetables and are a fair source of iron and Vitamin B (Niacin).

4 SERVINGS. *Per serving, 20 mg. sodium and 219 calories.*

MUSHROOMS MARJORAM

1 *lb. mushrooms*	1 *teaspoon vinegar*
2 *tablespoons water*	*Pepper to taste*
3 *tablespoons olive oil*	½ *teaspoon marjoram*
1 *clove garlic*	

Wash and cut mushrooms in large pieces. Heat water, oil in frying pan. Add garlic, vinegar, pepper, and marjoram. Stir well and cook slowly about 15 minutes. Remove garlic before serving.

4 SERVINGS. *Per serving, 4 mg. sodium and 101 calories.*

STUFFED MUSHROOMS

½ lb. mushrooms	1 minced medium onion
¼ cup melted unsalted butter or margarine	1 tablespoon sherry

Wash mushrooms and remove stems. Brush mushrooms with butter or margarine. Place in baking pan and broil four inches from heat until browned. Chop stems. Add stems and onion to remaining butter or margarine. Cook until well browned. Add sherry, mix well. Fill mushrooms with mixture. Broil 5 minutes or until mixture is lightly browned.

4 SERVINGS. *Per serving, 4 mg. sodium and 118 calories.*

MUSHROOMS WITH RICE

Mushrooms have been cultivated in Europe for over four hundred years, and their use goes back at least to Roman times.

1 lb. fresh mushrooms, sliced	3 low-sodium bouillon cubes, mixed with 3 cups boiling water
1 cup rice	
1 cup chopped tomatoes	½ cup red wine
½ cup onion, chopped	⅛ teaspoon pepper
½ cup unsalted butter or margarine	¼ teaspoon basil
	1 cup cooked fresh peas
	¼ cup grated low-sodium cheese

In a large skillet, cook rice, tomatoes, mushrooms, and onions in butter or margarine for about 10 minutes, stirring occasionally. Add bouillon mixture, wine, and seasonings; mix well. Cover. Simmer for 45 minutes or until rice is tender and liquid absorbed. Stir in peas. Sprinkle with cheese, heat again.

6 SERVINGS. *Per serving, 26 mg. sodium and 258 calories.*

MUSHROOMS WITH WINE ON TOAST

1 *lb. fresh mushrooms*	*Pepper to taste*
2 *tablespoons unsalted butter or margarine*	1 *teaspoon finely chopped marjoram*
2 *tablespoons olive oil or vegetable oil*	2 *tablespoons dry white wine*
1 *clove garlic, finely minced*	

Wash and thinly slice the mushrooms. Heat the butter or margarine and oil, and cook the garlic briefly without letting it brown. Add the mushrooms and cook 6 or 7 minutes, stirring occasionally. Sprinkle with pepper and marjoram. Add the wine and simmer one minute longer. Serve on low-sodium buttered toast.

4 SERVINGS. *Per serving, 5 mg. sodium and 129 calories.*

ONIONS

You can either boil onions or steam them. Take your choice. If you want to boil, place the peeled onions in a pan, cover with boiling water, and cook 30 to 45 minutes. If you like to steam, place unpeeled onions on rack over hot water. Cover the pan and steam away for 30 to 45 minutes. Then you have to peel. Probably no tears. If you boil, you can peel onions under cold running water. Here's your chance to use salt—and the only time in this book—rub your hands with salt or vinegar. No odor.

1 medium onion, 6 mg. sodium and 25 calories.

You may add to steam or boil the last 10 minutes:

1. ¼ *teaspoon basil*
   ¼ *teaspoon marjoram*
   ¼ *teaspoon thyme*

2. ¼ *teaspoon coriander*
   ¼ *teaspoon caraway*
       seed

Always pepper to taste. Add melted unsalted butter or margarine.

4 SERVINGS.

BAKED ONIONS AND APPLES

We had this for a company meal the other night. Annie was here to help me! She said, "These are delicious." Wish everyone could know Annie. Such a fine person and a wonderful assistant when my children were little.

2 *medium to large onions sliced ½ inch thick*
4 *cups apple rings ¼ inch thick*
½ *cup sugar*
¼ *teaspoon nutmeg*

¼ *teaspoon thyme*
1 *teaspoon grated lemon rind*
2 *tablespoons lemon juice*
¼ *cup unsalted butter or margarine*

Place a layer of sliced onions in an oiled baking dish, cover onions with a layer of apple rings, which should be cored but not peeled. Mix together the sugar, nutmeg, thyme, and lemon rind, and sprinkle over the apples. Repeat the process until onions and apples are used up. Pour over the top the lemon juice and melted butter or margarine and then bake for 1 hour in 350-degree oven.

4 SERVINGS. *Per serving, 9 mg. sodium and 316 calories.*

BERMUDA ONION IN FOIL

This recipe was given me flying over the Rockies. Ah! Low-sodium, I thought. I tried it the first night home.

1 *Bermuda onion*	2 *teaspoons sherry*
1 *teaspoon unsalted butter or margarine*	⅛ *teaspoon thyme*

Core onion as you would an apple. Be careful not to go all the way through. Fill cavity with butter or margarine, sherry, and thyme. Wrap in two thicknesses of aluminum foil. You may cook onion over charcoal or in oven until tender.

1 SERVING. *Total recipe, 17 mg. of sodium and 128 calories.*

GLAZED ONIONS

The characteristic odor of an onion is caused by a volatile oil which is removed by cooking. If you don't know what volatile means, I'll tell you—something that evaporates quickly.

3 *lbs. white onions, peeled*	6 *tablespoons unsalted butter or margarine*
4 *teaspoons sugar*	½ *teaspoon thyme*
1 *teaspoon dry mustard*	*Paprika*

Cook onions until tender (20 to 30 minutes), drain, put in shallow baking dish. Combine sugar, mustard, butter or margarine, and thyme. Spread mixture on onions. Sprinkle with paprika. Bake at 325 degrees for 20 minutes. Baste occasionally.

8 SERVINGS. *Per serving, 9 mg. sodium and 153 calories.*

PEAS

Remember to use only fresh peas. Frozen peas are usually salted. Never take chances. Two lbs. of unhulled peas make about two cupfuls and serves 4.

Cook peas in small amount of boiling water in a covered saucepan until tender.

½ cup peas, 0.7 mg. sodium and 56 calories.

Add to water with these variations:

1. *Lettuce leaf*
   ½ teaspoon sugar
   ½ teaspoon dried mint or dill (ground or seed)

2. *½ cup chopped onions. When cooked and drained add 1 tablespoon cream and 1 tablespoon unsalted butter or margarine*

3. *½ teaspoon lemon juice*
   ½ teaspoon sugar or 1 teaspoon honey

4. *3 pea pods. When cooked and drained add 2 tablespoons mint jelly (pure— without added preservatives) and 1 tablespoon unsalted butter or margarine*

4 SERVINGS.

HERBED PEAS

2 *lbs. fresh peas*
4 *tablespoons unsalted butter or margarine*
6 *green onions*
1 *tablespoon fresh chopped parsley*

¼ *teaspoon marjoram*
¼ *teaspoon rosemary*
⅛ *teaspoon thyme*
½ *teaspoon sugar*
4 *tablespoons cream*

Melt butter or margarine in heavy skillet. Add peas, onions, and all ingredients except cream. Cook covered until peas are tender, add cream, and heat thoroughly.

4 SERVINGS. *Per serving, 10 mg. sodium and 213 calories.*

PEAS A LA LOW-SODIUM

2 lbs. fresh peas
3 to 6 lettuce leaves
1 teaspoon sugar
⅛ teaspoon pepper

⅛ teaspoon savory
2 tablespoons unsalted
 butter or margarine

Line skillet with lettuce leaves. Add peas, sugar, pepper, and savory. Dot the top with butter or margarine. Cook tightly covered over medium heat 10 to 15 minutes. Do not overcook.

4 SERVINGS. *Per serving, 4 mg. sodium and 111 calories.*

PEAS AND MUSHROOMS

2 lbs. fresh peas
Lettuce leaf
½ lb. mushrooms, sliced
1 clove garlic
2 tablespoons vegetable
 oil

1 tablespoon flour
⅓ cup liquor from peas
Pepper
Parsley

Cook peas with lettuce leaf. Drain. Save liquor. Sauté in skillet mushrooms, garlic, and oil. Remove mushrooms and add to peas. Add to skillet 1 tablespoon flour and liquor from peas. Stir until smooth. Add peas and mushrooms. Season with pepper and garnish with chopped parsley if you wish.

4 SERVINGS. *Per serving, 4 mg. sodium and 133 calories.*

BAKED ACORN SQUASH

Nutmeg and acorn squash go together. I always thought that nutmeg trees grew in Connecticut, but the nutmeg state was deceiving me. It seems the early settlers were deceived too. Yankee peddlers made little wooden replicas of a nutmeg and sold them for a great price. They really did have the Charter Oak.

3 *acorn squash*	3 *teaspoons brown sugar*
1 *teaspoon nutmeg or ginger*	6 *teaspoons unsalted butter or margarine*
Pepper to taste	6 *teaspoons sweet sherry*

Split the squash in half and scoop out the fiber and seeds. Sprinkle the cavities with nutmeg or ginger, pepper, brown sugar, and butter or margarine. Place in a baking dish and bake 30 to 45 minutes in 325-degree oven or until tender. Five minutes before serving add sherry.

6 SERVINGS. *Per serving, 3 mg. sodium and 94 calories.*

BAKED ACORN SQUASH WITH APPLES

2 *small acorn squash*	*Nutmeg to taste*
4 *chopped apples*	2 *tablespoons unsalted butter or margarine*
4 *tablespoons brown sugar*	

Cut squash in halves and scoop out seeds. Place squash in a baking dish, fill centers with apple, pour a little water into the dish, cover, and bake at 350 degrees for 30 minutes or until partly done. Sprinkle with sugar and nutmeg and dot with butter or margarine. Bake uncovered about 45 minutes, or until squash is soft. I used brown sugar in this because it is a small amount. A dash of sherry is good.

4 SERVINGS. *Per serving, 6 mg. sodium and 216 calories.*

TOMATOES

Tomatoes are fine cooked with:

¼ teaspoon basil	¼ teaspoon oregano
1 bay leaf	1 teaspoon sugar
¼ teaspoon chervil	

Put in the whole works if you wish. You can always add a little flour to thicken. Pepper to taste. Chopped onions, a little garlic, or green pepper may be added. A sprinkle of thyme is good with fresh tomatoes.

4 SERVINGS. *4 fresh tomatoes (stewed), 12 mg. sodium and 120 calories. ½ cup canned low-sodium tomatoes, 7 mg. sodium and 25 calories.*

BAKED TOMATOES

4 medium tomatoes	Pepper to taste
1 tablespoon wheat germ	1 teaspoon basil
1 tablespoon unsalted butter or margarine	1 teaspoon sugar

Cut off stem ends. Place tomatoes in baking dish, mix wheat germ, butter or margarine, pepper, basil, and sugar. Sprinkle on top of tomatoes. Cover and bake at 375 degrees for about 30 minutes or until tomatoes are soft.

4 SERVINGS. *Per serving, 2 mg. sodium and 62 calories.*

TOMATOES IN FOIL

4 large tomatoes
Pepper to taste
8 teaspoons unsalted
  butter or margarine
¼ cup chopped parsley
⅓ cup chopped green
  onions including tops, or
  ⅓ cup onions

1 teaspoon basil
1 teaspoon tarragon
1 clove garlic, minced

Cut tomatoes crosswise into halves. Sprinkle with pepper, top each with 1 teaspoon butter or margarine. Mix remaining ingredients and mound equally on each tomato half. Set tomatoes on 2 pieces of aluminum foil. Wrap and seal tightly. Grill on charcoal or bake in oven until soft.

4 SERVINGS. *Per serving, 6 mg. sodium and 106 calories.*

TOMATOES SCALLOPED

This is great, because you can make it the day before, and it is also very compatible with masculine interest— you know, steaks, chops, or chicken.

1 lb. mushrooms
1 onion, diced
2 tablespoons unsalted
  butter or margarine
2 tablespoons flour

1 teaspoon basil
Pepper to taste
2 cups canned low-sodium
  tomatoes

Sauté mushrooms and onion in butter or margarine. Sift flour over mushrooms. Season with basil and pepper. Add tomatoes. Put in greased casserole. Bake slowly 1½ hours.

Next day wonderful. All you have to do is make a salad, broil meat or chicken, and set the table. Sprinkle a little wheat germ on top of the casserole and dot with 2 tablespoons unsalted butter or margarine and a sprinkle of parsley—now reheat for use.

4 SERVINGS. *Per serving, 16 mg. sodium and 163 calories.*

HERBED TOMATO JUICE

You can convert this into an aspic if you add gelatin.

4 *cups canned low-sodium   ¼ teaspoon oregano*
  tomato juice   *½ teaspoon sugar*
½ *bay leaf*   *¼ teaspoon basil*
¼ *teaspoon dill*   *2 teaspoons lemon juice*
¼ *teaspoon marjoram*

Combine ingredients. Let stand at least 1 hour in refrigerator. Strain. Serve ice cold.

6 SERVINGS. *Per serving, 8 mg. sodium and 38 calories.*

ZUCCHINI CASSEROLE

This could cheer a weary meal.

4 *medium zucchini*   *½ teaspoon basil*
4 *large tomatoes*   *½ teaspoon oregano*
2 *medium chopped onions   2 teaspoons lemon juice*
1½ *cloves minced   4 tablespoons olive oil*
  garlic   *1 tablespoon chopped*
1 *chopped green pepper   parsley*

Combine tomatoes, skinned, peeled, and cut-up, onions, garlic, green pepper, basil, oregano, and lemon juice, and cook until thick. Cut squash into thick slices, brown on both sides in olive oil. Add squash and oil to tomato sauce. Sprinkle with parsley. Cook until zucchini is done and thick sauce remains. The squash does not have to be fried first, but the browning takes some of the excess juice and makes it tastier.

6 SERVINGS. *Per serving, 5 mg. sodium and 135 calories.*

ZUCCHINI WITH HERBS AND TOMATOES

. I buy my zucchini squash from an Italian couple. On their first Sunday in America, over fifty years ago, they all went to church. It wasn't their kind of church. They learned there was more than one kind of church in America and the next Sunday found where they belonged.

4 *medium zucchini*	½ *teaspoon oregano*
3 *tablespoons olive oil*	*Pepper to taste*
1 *small onion, chopped*	⅓ *cup hot water*
1 *clove garlic, minced*	1 *teaspoon sugar*
1 *bay leaf*	2 *peeled tomatoes, cut up*
1 *teaspoon basil*	

Wash and cut zucchini into thin rounds without peeling. Pour oil in frying pan, add onion and garlic, and cook 10 minutes without browning. Add squash, all herbs, and pepper. Stir and add water. Cover and cook 10 minutes. Add sugar and tomatoes, and cook until tender.

6 SERVINGS. *Per serving, 3 mg. sodium and 103 calories.*

MARINATED ZUCCHINI

A wonderful pickle substitute.

4 *medium zucchini*	1 *tablespoon chopped*
⅛ *cup olive oil*	*fresh parsley*
1 *clove garlic, chopped*	¼ *teaspoon pepper*
1 *teaspoon basil*	¼ *cup vinegar*
1 *teaspoon oregano*	

Cut zucchini into 1-inch slices. Sauté in hot oil until light brown, and drain on absorbent paper. In a casserole place one layer of zucchini. Dot with chopped garlic, basil, oregano, and parsley. Sprinkle with pepper. Repeat until all zucchini are used. Boil vinegar five minutes and pour over squash. Let marinate at least twelve hours. Drain and serve. Can be kept for over a week in refrigerator.

8 SERVINGS. *Per serving, 2 mg. sodium and 51 calories.*

BAKED SLICED POTATOES

Idaho was one of the first states to adopt woman suffrage (1896). Probably before the potato adopted Idaho.

Scrub and dry medium Idaho potatoes. Cut ¼-inch vertical slices, but don't cut through to bottom of potato. Place thin slices of onion between potato slices. Brush with unsalted butter or margarine, season with dash of pepper, garlic powder, mint, or rosemary. Wrap each potato in aluminum foil. Bake over hot charcoal fire or in a 450-degree oven for 45 to 60 minutes.

Potato, 40 mg. sodium and 97 calories.
½ onion, 3 mg. sodium and 13 calories.
1 tablespoon margarine, 1.5 mg. sodium and 100 calories.

1 SERVING.

STUFFED BAKED POTATOES

These are always compatible with masculine interests.

2 *baking potatoes*   4 *tablespoons milk*
1 *tablespoon unsalted*   *Pepper to taste*
  butter or margarine

Bake potatoes in hot oven, 450 degrees for 45 to 60 minutes. Remove potatoes from oven and cut in halves lengthwise. Scoop out the contents with a teaspoon. Mash, add butter or margarine, pepper, and milk. Beat until fluffy, pile lightly into shells, bake at 450 degrees for 15 minutes.

4 SERVINGS. *Per serving, 10 mg. sodium and 84 calories.*

Choose one of the following combinations for Stuffed or Baked Potatoes:

1. ½ *tablespoon low-sodium grated cheese*

2. 1 *teaspoon grated onion*

3. 1 *teaspoon chopped chives*

4. 2 *mushrooms sautéed and cut in pieces*

5. ½ *teaspoon curry powder or ½ teaspoon nutmeg*

6. 1 *tablespoon sour cream, 1 teaspoon chives, and 1 teaspoon grated onion*

MASHED POTATOES

Wish I had discovered this years ago.

4 *medium-sized potatoes*
1 *small onion, minced*
½ *clove garlic*
1 *bay leaf*
¼ *teaspoon rosemary*

2 *teaspoons chopped parsley*
1 *tablespoon unsalted butter or margarine*
3 *tablespoons hot milk*
⅛ *teaspoon mace*

Cook potatoes in saucepan in enough boiling water to which have been added onion, garlic, bay leaf, rosemary, and parsley. Cover and cook 20 to 40 minutes. Remove garlic and bay leaf. Drain, mash with fork, add butter or margarine, hot milk, and mace. Beat until creamy. Garnish with parsley.

4 SERVINGS. *Per serving, 11 mg. sodium and 134 calories.*

BOILED NEW POTATOES

Ah! Spring.

16 new potatoes, peeled or unpeeled	½ teaspoon dried mint
2 teaspoons chopped parsley	2 tablespoons unsalted butter or margarine
	¼ teaspoon nutmeg

Cook potatoes with parsley and mint in boiling water in covered saucepan for 20 to 30 minutes. Serve with melted butter or margarine and nutmeg.

4 SERVINGS. *Per serving, 5 mg. sodium and 147 calories.*

PARSLEY POTATOES

Parsley has been appreciated since the middle ages as a seasoning and a garnish in cooking. It contains Vitamins A and C, plus iron and iodine. So eat your garnish.

4 medium-sized peeled potatoes, cooked	⅛ teaspoon tarragon
4 tablespoons unsalted butter or margarine	⅛ teaspoon dry mustard
1 clove garlic	2 teaspoons chopped parsley
⅛ teaspoon thyme	Pepper to taste
⅛ teaspoon rosemary	½ teaspoon lemon juice

Melt butter or margarine. Add garlic. Remove from heat and let stand 5 to 10 minutes. Add thyme, rosemary, tarragon, mustard, parsley, pepper, and lemon juice. Let stand for at least ½ hour. Strain, reheat, and serve on hot potatoes.

4 SERVINGS. *Per serving, 6 mg. sodium and 197 calories.*

POTATOES WITH HERBS

This is one of the first mixtures I made. I should bury it in my file and give something else a turn.

4 *potatoes*	¼ *teaspoon allspice*
⅓ *cup flour*	*Pepper to taste*
½ *teaspoon thyme*	1 *clove garlic*
½ *teaspoon marjoram*	1 *bay leaf*

Start oven at 450 degrees and grease a shallow casserole with butter or margarine. Peel potatoes and cut in quarters. Now mix flour, thyme, marjoram, allspice, and pepper. Dip potatoes in this mixture and place in casserole. Toss in garlic clove and bay leaf. Dot with butter or margarine. Cover tightly. Bake 40 minutes or until potatoes are tender.

4 SERVINGS. *Per serving, 6 mg. sodium and 204 calories.*

HASH-BROWNED POTATOES

2 *cups diced cooked potatoes*	¼ *teaspoon rosemary*
	2 *tablespoons milk*
4 *tablespoons finely chopped onion*	2 *tablespoons vegetable or olive oil*
4 *teaspoons flour*	⅛ *teaspoon nutmeg*
Pepper to taste	

Combine potatoes and onion. Mix flour, pepper, and rosemary. Slowly blend in milk. Combine with the potato and onion mixture. Heat oil in heavy frying pan. Spread potato mixture evenly in the pan, making one large cake that does not touch the sides.

Cook over medium heat until the under side is brown. Cut into four equal portions and turn each piece to brown on other side. Sprinkle with nutmeg.

4 SERVINGS. *Per serving, 9 mg. sodium and 172 calories.*

Try caraway seeds sprinkled over French fried potatoes.

POTATOES COOKED IN FOIL

6 *potatoes cut in halves*   2 *teaspoons dried mint*
2 *tablespoons unsalted*   *Pepper to taste*
  butter or margarine

Place potatoes on two pieces of aluminum foil. Spread
with butter or margarine, mint, and pepper. Fold foil over
and turn over edges. Bake in oven at 375 degrees for 35 to
40 minutes.
6 SERVINGS. *Per serving, 4 mg. sodium and 130 calories.*

LYONNAISE POTATOES

After all these years I looked up the word *Lyonnaise*. It
means a method of slicing cold boiled potatoes and frying
with onions and serving garnished with parsley. Anyway,
they are good and we will add the rosemary. Don't tell the
Lyonnais. In *Hamlet,* Ophelia said, "There's rosemary,
that's for remembrance."

4 *cold, boiled potatoes*   *Pepper to taste*
1 *medium onion sliced*   ¼ *teaspoon rosemary*
  fine   *Parsley*
4 *tablespoons unsalted*
  butter or margarine

Fry the onion in the butter or margarine and cook until
light brown. Slice the potatoes thin, sprinkle them with
pepper and rosemary. Place in the frying pan and cook
with onion until a rich golden brown. Garnish with parsley.
4 SERVINGS. *Per serving, 7 mg. sodium and 203 calories.*

BAKED SWEET POTATOES

Wash and dry sweet potatoes of medium size. Bake until tender in a hot oven (425 degrees). If you want the skin to be soft, rub a little unsalted butter or margarine on before baking.

Now comes the fun and a gay and good delight for the salty as well as the unsalty. Cut crisscross gashes in the skin of the baked potato, then pinch them so that some of the soft inside pops through the opening, drop in one of the following:

1. 1 *tablespoon low-sodium peanut butter or 8 chopped roasted peanuts; then add 1 tablespoon orange juice*

2. 1 *tablespoon unsalted butter or margarine plus a dash of nutmeg and sherry*

3. 1 *tablespoon honey* 1 *tablespoon unsalted butter or margarine*

1 medium sweet potato, 12.0 mg. sodium and 183 calories.

1 tablespoon low-sodium peanut butter, 7.0 mg. sodium and 100 calories.

1 tablespoon honey, 1.5 mg. sodium and 62 calories.

1 tablespoon unsalted butter or margarine, 1.5 mg. sodium and 100 calories.

1 SERVING.

GLAZED SWEET POTATOES

We think this is a delectable, easy dish and will cheer a holiday meal. Like honey bees, the unsalty will be in clover.

4 *sweet potatoes*
  (*medium*)
¼ *teaspoon nutmeg*
6 *tablespoons honey*

4 *teaspoons unsalted*
  butter or margarine
2 *oranges*

Pare sweet potatoes and cut in half. Drop into enough boiling water to just cover. Add nutmeg, honey, butter or margarine. Cover and boil until potatoes are tender. If liquid has not cooked down enough by the time they are tender, remove cover and boil rapidly until a syrup is formed. Baste sweet potatoes occasionally with the syrup. Garnish with sliced oranges.

4 SERVINGS. *Per serving, 17 mg. sodium and 313 calories.*

HOT FRUIT AND SWEET POTATO

A fine dish for a party, with sliced cold turkey an exciting colleague.

4 *medium sweet potatoes*
1 *medium can peaches*
1 *medium can pears*
1 *medium can pineapple*
1 *medium can apricots*

½ *cup unsalted butter or*
  margarine
¾ *cup brown sugar*
4 *teaspoons curry*

Cook potatoes. Peel and slice in ½-inch slices. Drain peaches, pears, pineapple, and apricots. Place all in layers in ovenproof dish and add melted butter or margarine. Sprinkle with sugar and curry. Bake for 1 hour in 350-degree oven.

10 SERVINGS. *Per serving, 17 mg. sodium and 313 calories.*

SCALLOPED SWEET POTATOES

This recipe can grow or shrink, according to the number of family or guests, so you figure out the sodium content. It will be good for you.

1 medium sweet potato, 12 mg. sodium and 183 calories.

1 medium apple, 2 mg. sodium and 75 calories.

1 medium orange, 2 mg. sodium and 70 calories.

1 cup canned cranberry sauce, 2.5 mg. sodium and 548 calories.

1 tablespoon low-sodium margarine, 1.5 mg. sodium and 100 calories.

1 cup sugar, 0.8 mg. sodium and 770 calories.

Place alternate layers of sliced cooked sweet potatoes and sliced raw apples in a baking dish greased with vegetable oil. Sprinkle the apple layers with sugar, nutmeg, and a dot of unsalted margarine. Add just enough hot water to cover bottom of dish. Bake covered in oven 375 degrees, 30 to 40 minutes. For variety, try peeled orange slices or cranberry sauce instead of apples.

SWEET POTATOES FRIED WITH APPLES

We seem to be carried away by sweet potatoes. These have a country-kitchen look.

3 medium raw sweet potatoes, sliced and peeled

3 raw apples (leave skins on)

3 tablespoons unsalted butter or margarine

5 tablespoons honey

¼ teaspoon nutmeg or fennel seed

1 teaspoon sherry

Place potatoes and apples in a hot frying pan with

melted butter or margarine. Add honey, cover, cook over low heat until tender or lightly brown, about 30 minutes. Turn occasionally, sprinkle with a little nutmeg or fennel seed and sherry.

4 SERVINGS. *Per serving, 14 mg. sodium and 348 calories.*

OVEN-COOKED RICE

2 *cups boiling water*
1 *cup rice*
2 *tablespoons lemon juice*
1 *tablespoon unsalted butter or margarine*

2 *teaspoons chopped parsley*
⅛ *teaspoon cumin*

Mix ingredients and pour into greased casserole. Cover and bake 35 to 45 minutes in 350-degree oven.

4 SERVINGS. *Per serving, 2 mg. sodium and 199 calories.*

LEMON-PARSLEY RICE

¼ *cup vegetable oil*
3 *tablespoons fresh parsley, minced*

1 *tablespoon lemon juice*

Mix and pour over hot cooked rice.

4 SERVINGS. *Per serving, 1 mg. sodium and 252 calories.*

Honey and brown sugar are fine over rice. You will also like hot fruit over rice.

ORANGE-FLAVORED RICE

Good with duck, chicken, or pork dishes.

1 *cup rice*
1 *cup water (cold)*
1 *cup orange juice*

2 *teaspoons grated orange rind*
1 *teaspoon unsalted butter or margarine*

Combine rice, water, orange juice, orange rind, butter or margarine in heavy 3-quart saucepan. Turn heat high until rice starts to boil. Stir once with fork. Reduce heat, cover and simmer 12 to 14 minutes until liquid is absorbed. You may have to add a bit more orange juice if rice is not moist enough.

4 SERVINGS. *Per serving, 4 mg. sodium and 216 calories.*

TOMATO-FLAVORED RICE

As I have been writing this book, rice has become an obsession with me. I have tried rice in all kinds of ways, mixed with all kinds of odd things. Anyway, it has been a challenge. Try these.

1 *cup rice*
1 *cup water (cold)*
1 *cup canned low-sodium tomato juice*

1 *tablespoon unsalted butter or margarine*
2 *teaspoons minced onion*
½ *teaspoon basil*

Combine rice, water, tomato juice, butter or margarine, onion, and basil in heavy 3-quart saucepan. Turn heat to high until rice starts to boil. Stir once with fork. Reduce heat, cover, and simmer 12 to 14 minutes until liquid is absorbed. You may have to add a bit more tomato juice if rice is not moist enough.

4 SERVINGS. *Per serving, 5 mg. sodium and 209 calories.*

WAIKIKI RICE

The original recipe called for brown sugar, but we substituted white. If you have been careful on your count today use brown if you like. The sodium content of 1 tablespoon of white sugar is negligible, but 1 tablespoon of brown sugar has 3.4 mg.

1⅓ cups water
1 cup canned pineapple tidbits
¼ cup white sugar
⅛ teaspoon ground cloves

2 tablespoons unsalted butter or margarine
1⅓ cups quick-cooking rice

Bring all ingredients except rice to a boil. Stir in rice. Cover and simmer 10 minutes. Aloha!

4 SERVINGS. *Per serving, 3 mg. sodium and 377 calories.*

BAKED BEANS

2 cups pea beans
1 bay leaf
½ cup white sugar
2 tablespoons brown sugar
¾ cup chopped onion
2 teaspoons dry mustard
1 teaspoon low-sodium prepared mustard

2 teaspoons low-sodium Worcestershire sauce
2 cups canned low-sodium tomatoes
¼ teaspoon pepper
¼ cup unsalted butter or margarine

Cook beans according to directions on package *without salt* but with bay leaf. Drain, reserving bean water. Combine sugars, onion, mustards, Worcestershire sauce, tomatoes, and pepper. Add 1½ cups of bean water. Pour into greased covered casserole. Dot with butter or margarine. Bake 6 to 8 hours in 250-degree oven. Add more bean water if beans become dry. Uncover for last hour of cooking.

8 SERVINGS. *Per serving, 7 mg. sodium and 284 calories.*

FRIED APPLES

6 *apples*	¼ *cup hot water*
3 *tablespoons unsalted*	¼ *cup sugar*
butter or margarine	½ *teaspoon cinnamon*

Wash and core apples. Cut in very thin quarters. Put in pan with hot butter or margarine. Brown on both sides. Add water, sugar, and cinnamon. Cover and steam for twenty minutes.

4 SERVINGS. *Per serving, 4 mg. sodium and 235 calories.*

BAKED ORANGES

Serve this on Halloween or whenever.

Select medium oranges. Wash, simmer whole oranges in plenty of water in covered kettle until toothpick pierces skin easily. Drain, cut in halves or quarters, put in baking dish. Make syrup in proportion—1 cup sugar, ¾ cup water (enough to cover oranges). Bake in moderate oven 350 degrees for 45 minutes or until oranges look translucent. Turn oranges while baking or while cooling in syrup.

1 medium orange, 2 mg. sodium and 70 calories.
1 cup sugar, 0.8 mg. sodium and 770 calories.

BAKED BANANAS

Place bananas in a buttered baking dish. Sprinkle each banana with a few drops of lemon juice, then spread with 1 teaspoon of honey. We like to add a little nutmeg and top the banana with a little unsalted butter or margarine. This is wonderful served with yams or sweet potatoes accompanied by broiled pineapple and apple slices.

1 banana, 1.4 mg. sodium and 99 calories.

1 teaspoon honey, 0.5 mg. sodium and 21 calories.

1 tablespoon low-sodium butter or margarine, 1.5 mg. sodium and 100 calories.

1 SERVING.

24 Christmas, Thanksgiving, and Other Goodies

Christmas, Thanksgiving, and Other Goodies

I had not yet made a low-sodium pie for our "first Thanksgiving." There were too many other things to learn. So there was no pumpkin pie. I read that the Pilgrims had many things to learn, too, so they didn't have pumpkin pie until their second Thanksgiving. We had the beautiful fruits of the season. The most important part of our holiday tradition is not the pie or the fruit but the gathering of our family and the understanding of why we are observing these celebrated days.

Christmas and Thanksgiving can be full of "goodies" for unsalty. We wondered about our usual cookie recipes and found that our favorites contained so little salt that salt's omission would not alter their familiar taste.

PUMPKIN PIE

> *We have pumpkins at morning*
> *and pumpkins at noon,*
>
> *If it were not for pumpkins,*
> *we should be undone*
>
> AN EARLY PILGRIM

I was undone, too, trying to find a good recipe for pumpkin pie that was good for unsalty. Tried and tried until I discovered that it can be made without egg and milk.

1 baked low-sodium pie shell
1 tablespoon gelatin
¼ cup cold water
1½ cups cooked or canned pumpkin
¾ cup white or brown sugar
1 teaspoon cinnamon

2 teaspoons grated orange peel
½ teaspoon nutmeg
2 tablespoons rum or orange juice
2 tablespoons unsalted butter or margarine
½ cup chopped pecans

Soak gelatin in water for 5 minutes. Combine ingredients, and cook until slightly thickened. Pour in pie shell. Place a few pecans on top. Cool.

6 SERVINGS. *Per serving with crust, 10 mg. sodium and 461 calories with brown sugar. Per serving with crust, 3 mg. sodium and 455 calories with white sugar.*

GOOD APPLE PIE

Low-Sodium Pastry* for a 2-crust, 9-inch pie
4 cups greening apples
1 cup sugar
½ teaspoon cinnamon
½ teaspoon vanilla

Grated rind from ½ lemon
1 tablespoon lemon juice
1 tablespoon unsalted butter or margarine

Make the pastry. Line a 9-inch pie pan with pastry, saving the rest for top crust. Chill both in refrigerator while you prepare the filling. Heat oven to 450 degrees. Peel, core, and slice apples very thin. Mix sliced apples with sugar, cinnamon, vanilla, lemon rind and juice. Fill into unbaked pie shell. Dot with bits of butter or margarine and cover with top crust. Bake 10 minutes, then reduce heat to 350 degrees and continue baking 30 to 35 minutes more. During last 5 minutes of baking, brush pastry top with cream and sprinkle with granulated sugar.

6 SERVINGS. *Per serving with crust, 4 mg. sodium and 432 calories.*

CHERRY-APPLE PIE

Low-Sodium Pastry* for a
  2-crust pie
4 cups sliced, pared apples
1 tablespoon flour
⅓ cup sugar

1 tablespoon orange juice
3 tablespoons cherry
  preserves
½ teaspoon mace

Line 9-inch pie plate with half the pastry. Combine apples, flour, sugar, and orange juice, and pour mixture into shell. Spoon preserves over the filling and sprinkle with mace. Cover with remaining pastry. Slash the top. Bake 40 minutes in 400-degree oven.

6 SERVINGS. *Per serving with crust, 4 mg. sodium and 363 calories.*

DOUBLE-CRUST PIE DOUGH

2 cups sifted flour
¼ cup water
⅔ cup vegetable
  shortening
¼ teaspoon mace

½ teaspoon grated lemon
  rind
Add sesame seeds if you
  like them

Sift flour into bowl. Remove ⅓ cup of this flour and mix with water, forming a paste. Set aside.

Add vegetable shortening, mace, and lemon rind to flour, and cut mixture until pieces are the size of peas. Add paste mixture to flour mix and mix thoroughly until dough comes together and can be shaped into a ball. Divide into two parts. Chill. Roll ⅛ inch thick. Bake at 450 degrees for 15 to 20 minutes. Sesame seeds added to the dough add interest. Makes crust for 9-inch, 2-crust pie.

Total recipe, 6 mg. sodium and 1332 calories.

PASTRIES (GOOD)

So says our family and my loose-leaf cookbook.

You can bake gifts for your unsalty friends at Christmastime. What a treat! Place them in a shoe box covered with foil and tie a red ribbon with a little pine on top.

½ cup unsalted butter or margarine	1 cup bread flour
3 teaspoons confectioners' sugar	1 teaspoon vanilla
	¼ teaspoon mace

Cream butter or margarine and sugar. Add flour, vanilla, and mace. Put teaspoon of mixture into tiny cupcake tins. Press with finger tips into pan. Bake at 350 degrees for 45 minutes or until light brown.

To Fill

I just counted the dates in a package—54.

1 package dates	½ cup water
1 cup sugar	

Chop dates, combine ingredients, and cook until slightly thickened. Mixture thickens as it cools. Fill when cool. A jam or jelly may be used for filling too.

12 PASTRIES. *Per pastry, 2 mg. sodium and 102 calories. Per filling, negligible mg. sodium and 159 calories.*

PASTRY FOR TARTS

⅔ cup unsalted butter or
   margarine
½ cup sugar
⅛ teaspoon mace

2 egg yolks
2 cups sifted all-purpose
   flour

Blend butter or margarine, sugar, mace, egg yolks, and flour together. Divide into 12 pieces. Press each piece into 2-inch tart shells. Chill. Bake at 350 degrees—20 to 25 minutes. Fill with cooked fruit, jelly, or jam.

MAKES 12 TARTS. *Per tart, 4 mg. sodium and 143 calories.*

BROWNIES I

2 squares unsweetened
   chocolate
¼ cup unsalted butter or
   margarine
1 cup sugar

1 egg
½ cup flour
½ cup walnut meats,
   cut up
1 teaspoon vanilla

Melt the chocolate over hot water in saucepan. Remove pan from heat. Add the butter or margarine and stir until melted. Add sugar, egg, flour, nutmeats, and vanilla. Spread the mixture evenly in a 7-inch square shallow pan lined with heavy wax paper. Bake 1 hour in a slow oven, 300 degrees. Turn out on board and pull off the paper. Cut the brownies into squares while still warm.

MAKES 16 BROWNIES. *Per brownie, 5 mg. sodium and 131 calories.*

BROWNIES II

The addition of another egg to Brownies I makes quite a count difference.

2 *eggs, well beaten*
1 *cup sugar*
2 *squares unsweetened chocolate*

½ *cup unsalted butter or margarine*
½ *cup flour (scant)*
½ *cup walnut meats, cut up*

Beat eggs, add sugar. Melt butter or margarine with chocolate and combine with eggs and sugar and flour, add nuts. Pour in oiled pan and bake in 400-degree oven for 20 minutes.

MAKES 16 BROWNIES. *Per brownie, 10 mg. sodium and 161 calories.*

UNSALTY'S CHRISTMAS COOKIES

These are a delight.

1 *cup unsalted butter or margarine*
1 *cup sugar*
1 *egg yolk*
2 *cups sifted all-purpose flour*

2½ *teaspoons cinnamon*
¼ *teaspoon mace*
1 *egg white*
Ground nuts, unsalted

Cream butter or margarine and sugar thoroughly. Beat in egg yolk, add flour, cinnamon, and mace, and blend well. Roll pieces of the dough into 1-inch balls between buttered palms. Place balls about 2 inches apart on ungreased baking sheet. Press out paper-thin with a floured spatula. Paint with egg white and sprinkle with ground nuts. Bake at 350 degrees for 10 to 12 minutes.

MAKES 6 DOZEN. *Per cookie, 2 mg. sodium and 45 calories.*

PECAN PUFFS

½ cup unsalted butter or
   margarine
2 tablespoons granulated
   sugar
1 teaspoon vanilla

1 cup flour, sifted
1 cup pecan meats,
   ground
¼ teaspoon nutmeg
confectioners' sugar

Cream butter or margarine until soft and blend in granulated sugar until creamy. Add vanilla. Stir flour, pecans, and nutmeg into mixture. Roll dough into small balls and place on a well-greased cookie sheet. Bake in 300-degree oven for about 45 minutes. Roll puffs in confectioners' sugar while hot and again when cold.

MAKES 2 DOZEN. *Per cookie, 1 mg. sodium and 87 calories.*

LEMON-ORANGE CAKE (WONDERFUL)

Unsalty will love a tiny piece. Why do eggs and milk have to have so much sodium? Happy birthday to you!

3 beaten egg yolks
½ orange (juice and
   grated rind)
½ lemon (juice and
   grated rind)
1 cup sugar

1 tablespoon plus 1
   teaspoon flour
1 cup milk
3 stiffly beaten egg
   whites

Add egg yolks to juice and rind of orange and lemon. Beat well. Mix sugar and flour and add to mixture. Slowly stir in milk. Fold in stiffly beaten egg whites last. Pour in baking dish. Set in pan of hot water and bake at 350 degrees for 45 minutes. There will be a tasty lemon-orange custard at the bottom, with a layer of golden sponge cake on top.

10 SERVINGS. *Per serving, 33 mg. sodium and 110 calories.*

APPLE CRISP

What a wonderful fragrance!

4 *cups sliced apples*	½ *cup flour*
1 *cup water*	6 *tablespoons unsalted*
1 *teaspoon cinnamon*	*butter or margarine*
¾ *cup sugar*	

Peel and slice apples thin. Fill a low casserole with apples, water, and cinnamon. Blend rest of ingredients until crumbly, using knife. Spread this mixture on top of apples and bake uncovered for 1 hour in 400-degree oven.

6 SERVINGS. *Per serving, 2 mg. sodium and 294 calories.*

APPLE TAPIOCA

Tapioca has been regarded for years as a light and nutritious food, and it is tasty too.

2 *medium-sized apples*	2 *tablespoons quick-*
½ *cup sugar*	*cooking tapioca*
2 *cups water*	¼ *teaspoon nutmeg or*
	cinnamon

Pare and slice apples. Add sugar to the water, place over heat, and stir until sugar is dissolved. Add apples and cover pan. Cook slowly until apples are just tender—about 15 minutes. Carefully stir in tapioca and continue cooking a few minutes, until tapioca is transparent. Sprinkle with nutmeg or cinnamon. Cool.

4 SERVINGS. *Per serving, 2 mg. sodium and 150 calories.*

CRANBERRY APPLESAUCE

You can buy this combination in a can nowadays, but it contains no raisins or cinnamon.

2 cups jellied cranberry sauce	¼ cup raisins
	¼ teaspoon cinnamon
½ cup canned applesauce	¼ teaspoon allspice

Crush cranberry sauce with a fork. Stir in applesauce, raisins, cinnamon and allspice. Chill.

6 SERVINGS. *Per serving, 5 mg. sodium and 188 calories.*

BAKED APPLES

Nothing like the aroma of apples baking on a crisp autumn day. The word "aroma" comes from the ancient Greek word for spices.

4 apples	1 teaspoon nutmeg, mace, or cinnamon
8 tablespoons honey	
4 teaspoons grated orange peel	

Boil honey, orange peel, and nutmeg, mace, or cinnamon. Add apples. Cook about 5 minutes, turning apples often in syrup. Place apples in baking dish, spoon sauce over apples. Bake 15 to 20 minutes at 350 degrees, basting 2 or 3 times with sauce. Chill.

4 SERVINGS. *Per serving, 5 mg. sodium and 199 calories.*

CHERRIES JUBILEE

> "God bless us everyone."
> —Dickens, *A Christmas Carol*

These could be just as much a part of Christmas as a Christmas carol.

2½ cups canned, pitted black cherries	¼ cup sugar
	½ teaspoon cinnamon
2 thin slices lemon	½ cup brandy

Heat, but do not boil, cherries. Add juice with lemon in blazer pan or chafing dish. Mix sugar and cinnamon and sprinkle over the top. Add brandy, set ablaze. When flame dies out serve at once over Lemon-Orange Cake,* on special days.

8 SERVINGS. *Per serving, 2 mg. sodium and 123 calories.*

CHRISTMAS DESSERT

Certainly unsalty is allowed 1 tablespoon of whipped cream to celebrate.

½ cup canned apple and cranberry sauce (a lovely holiday red)	1 tablespoon whipped cream
½ teaspoon allspice	2 teaspoons creme de menthe

Use your prettiest sherbet glasses. Put in sauce mixed with allspice, and top with the whipped cream mixed with creme de menthe. Place sprig of holly on underneath plate.

This also can be used at Easter with canned peaches and garnished with tiny easter-egg candy for the salty.

1 SERVING. *Per serving, 10 mg. sodium and 254 calories.*

BAKED RHUBARB

A recipe of my mother's. Mother gave me most of my knowledge of nutrition and balanced meal planning. She made wonderful vegetable soup—too full of sodium to include in this book. Too bad.

2 *lbs. cut rhubarb*   1 *cup sugar*

Wash rhubarb in cold water. Do not peel. Now, Elma, use your kitchen scissors, so as not to tear. Cut stalks in 2-inch pieces. Place rhubarb and sugar in baking dish. Cover and place in preheated moderate oven for 20 minutes until sugar is melted. Remove cover and finish baking for 30 minutes in moderate oven. Mother typed this recipe when she was over 75 years old.

8 SERVINGS. *Per serving, 1 mg. sodium and 106 calories.*

CANTALOUPE OR HONEYDEW COOLER

This looks pretty.

Halve, seed, and peel the melon, cut in four wedges. Place on platter. Dip white seedless grapes in fruit juice and then roll in white sugar. Place grapes in small bunches on melon. Add mint for color. The Italians use this for a canapé. They serve it with Italian cheese that salty can have.

4 SERVINGS.
30 grapes, 3.5 mg. sodium and 70 calories.
1 melon, 24 mg. sodium and 72 calories.
Try a sprinkle of cardamom with fresh melon.

THRILLED[1]

16 *marshmallows*   1 *cup orange juice*

Heat juice and marshmallows until latter are dissolved. Cutting marshmallows into pieces hastens process. Pour into sherbet glasses and chill. Lemon juice and rind of lemon may be added.

4 SERVINGS. *Per serving, 14 mg. sodium and 107 calories.*

RICE PUDDING

1 *cup rice*   1 *cup white sugar*
3 *cups water*   ¼ *teaspoon cumin seed*
2 *lemons (juice)*   ½ *teaspoon cinnamon*

Boil rice and water in double boiler. When almost dry, mix with lemon juice, sugar, cumin seed, and cinnamon. Pour in mold. Serve cold with Vanilla Sauce.*

6 SERVINGS. *Per serving, 2 mg. sodium and 249 calories.*

PINEAPPLE SHERBET

2 *cups sugar*   1 *tablespoon cold water*
1 *quart boiling water*   2 *lemons (juice)*
¼ *teaspoon gelatin*   1 *can crushed pineapple*

Boil sugar and water 20 minutes. Soak gelatin 2 minutes in cold water. Add hot syrup gradually, until gelatin is

---

[1] When I discovered that one marshmallow only had 3.1 mg. of sodium.

dissolved. Let cool. Add lemon juice and canned pineapple. Stir and freeze.

6 SERVINGS. *Per serving, 1 mg. sodium and 331 calories.*

CRANBERRY SHERBET

Cranberries should be used all year. They are good for you. Try this on a hot summer day.

1 *envelope unflavored*	3 *cups cranberry juice*
gelatin	1 *cup sugar*
¼ *cup cold water*	3 *tablespoons lemon juice*

Sprinkle gelatin over cold water to soften. Heat 1 cup cranberry juice to boiling point, remove from heat. Stir in softened gelatin and sugar until both are dissolved. Add remaining 2 cups cranberry juice and lemon juice. Pour into ice-cube tray and place in freezing compartment. Freeze to mushy stage. Transfer to mixing bowl and beat until mixture is pink and smooth. Return to tray or trays and freeze until firm.

6 SERVINGS. *Per serving, 2 mg. sodium and 226 calories.*

LEMON ICE CREAM

3 *tablespoons lemon juice*	1 *cup low-sodium dry*
2 *teaspoons grated lemon*	*milk*
rind	1 *cup milk*
1 *cup sugar*	

Add lemon juice and rind to sugar, blending well. Slowly stir in milk. Place in ice-cube tray of refrigerator. Takes about 2 hours. Do not stir, and it will freeze smooth.

6 SERVINGS. *Per serving, 22 mg. sodium and 171 calories. Per serving (if whole milk is substituted for low-sodium dry milk), 40 mg. sodium and 185 calories.*

MISTAKES[2]

These *Mistakes* do have 3 egg whites, and you know they are high in sodium. Don't make another mistake by giving unsalty more than one or two. Unsalty should have treats once in a while, providing he stays within the count.

3 *egg whites*
3 *tablespoons powdered sugar*
1 *tablespoon vinegar*

1 *cup shredded coconut*
1 *cup chopped walnut meats*

Beat egg whites, sugar, and vinegar until stiff. Add coconut and nuts to make very stiff. Drop on greased pan and bake quickly in 350-degree oven for 6 to 8 minutes.
MAKES 24 COOKIES. *Per serving, 8 mg. sodium and 46 calories.*

ONE AND FIVE THREES

1 *large can crushed pineapple*
3 *pints water*
3 *cups sugar*

3 *lemons (juice)*
3 *oranges (juice)*
3 *bananas, mashed*

Boil sugar and water together 5 minutes. Add can of crushed pineapple using all the juice. Add rest of ingredients. Freeze in refrigerator tray, stirring well after it begins to freeze.
8 SERVINGS. *Per serving, 3 mg. sodium and 428 calories.*

---

[2] Not to have made more.

BRANDIED PEACHES

16 *canned peach halves*   9 *whole cloves*
3 *cups sugar*   ½ *cup brandy*
2 *2-inch sticks cinnamon*

Simmer syrup from can of peach halves with sugar, cinnamon, cloves for 5 minutes. Bring peaches to boil in this syrup and add brandy. Pour into covered jar. Keep at least one week before using.
Per peach (with sauce), 2 mg. sodium and 203 calories.

GRAPES WITH SOUR CREAM

30 *white seedless grapes*   1 *teaspoon brown sugar*
1 *tablespoon sour cream*

Place grapes in sherbet glass. Mix sour cream with sugar and mix with grapes. Chill in refrigerator for 4 hours.
1 SERVING. *Per serving, 11 mg. sodium and 136 calories.*

SPICED TOKAY GRAPES

1 *lb. Tokay grapes*   ¼ *teaspoon allspice*
1½ *cups sugar*   1 *tablespoon instant*
1 *cup cider vinegar*   *minced onion*
3 *3-inch sticks cinnamon*

Wash, then drain grapes, snip into small clusters. Place grapes in wide-mouthed jar. Mix sugar, vinegar, cinnamon, allspice, and onion together in a saucepan. Bring to boil and simmer a few minutes. Pour hot syrup over grapes, let stand several hours or overnight, stirring once or twice. (Serve as hors d'oeuvres or as an accompaniment to meat, fish, or poultry.)

4 SERVINGS. *Total recipe, 12 mg. sodium and 1324 calories.*

CANDIED WALNUTS

1½ cups sugar   3 *tablespoons orange juice*
¼ cup water

Cook to soft boil. Then add:

¼ to ½ cup grated   2½ *cups walnut meats*
   orange rind

Pour on wax paper to cool.

ABOUT 35 PIECES. *Total recipe, 8 mg. sodium and 3044 calories.*

UNSALTY'S APRICOT CANDY

2 *cups dried apricots*   1 *cup sugar*
   (read label)   ¾ *cup water*

Soak the apricots 15 minutes. Make a syrup of the sugar and water. When it boils drop in drained apricots and cook for 5 minutes. Lay apricots on wax paper. When they are dry, roll in granulated sugar. Chill.

MAKES 40 PIECES. *Per apricot candy, 1 mg. sodium and 35 calories.*

SPICED NUTS

1 *cup sugar*
⅓ *teaspoon cinnamon*
6 *tablespoons milk*

½ *teaspoon vanilla*
1¾ *cups nuts*

Cook first 3 ingredients without stirring to soft-ball stage. Remove from stove, add vanilla and nuts. Stir until mixture begins to thicken. Turn out on wax paper and separate nuts.

ABOUT 25 PIECES. *Total recipe, 51 mg. sodium and 2129 calories. Per piece, 2 mg. sodium and 86 calories.*

STARLIKE STRAWBERRY PRESERVES

4 *cups whole strawberries*
3 *cups sugar*

⅓ *cup lemon juice,*
strained

Stem berries and remove spots. Wash and drain. Put berries in saucepan with sugar. Let stand 12 hours. Place over low fire, and when it comes to rolling boil, let it boil 8 to 10 minutes. Add lemon juice and cook 2 more minutes. Remove scum. Set aside to cool so that berries will be distributed throughout the glass. When cool put in sterilized glasses. Put paraffin over twice for sealing.

MAKES 1½ PINTS. *Total recipe, 13 mg. sodium and 2539 calories. Per tablespoon, sodium negligible and 63 calories.*

A Note to Unsalty

Although, as you have learned by now, sugar is very low in sodium nevertheless it also has a very high caloric content and it is best that you limit the use of very sweet desserts to a special occasion and then just enjoy a small portion. Try instead the lovely fruits of the season.

25 Cattail Parties and
What Goes with Them

A friend of ours asked Susan, when she was little, where her parents had gone, and she announced, "To a cattail party." Cattail, cocktail, or tea party, depending on your tastes and what you do when you get there, are all acceptable names.

There was a time in our lives, not too long ago (we like to think), when we were most interested in the refreshments and the prizes at parties. It is not much different in adult life. We do show more interest in someone else's dress or the V.I.P. who honored us with polite words. But most of us, salty and unsalty alike, enjoy congenial friends and good stimulating conversation. How well they go along with festive foods and mood! Most hors d'oeuvres and canapés are on the big NO list for unsalty. One large olive has 156 mg. of sodium, anchovy paste has 686 mg. of sodium per teaspoon, and 1 dill pickle has 1900 mg. Unbelievable, isn't it, in comparison to an apple with 2 mg. of sodium. So there again, you take with you more and varied sneak-ins. Just fix a plateful of goodies on your best china, and away you go. Make enough so the salties can share. If there is "help" in the kitchen, explain, and leave the plate with her. Otherwise, no problem. Leave the plate on the coffee table. Unsalty becomes very popular with the salties. They need to lose weight (so they say).

I would like to share our finds with you. You can buy fine, tasty low-sodium melba toast and rounds at most grocery stores or supermarkets. There are some good thin

189

wafers too. If they are not on the shelves, ask your store-keeper to order some. He will. He likes your business. We have also discovered wonderful unsalted potato chips cooked in vegetable oil. If your potato-chip man doesn't make them, start him making them.

Raw vegetables and fruits are wonderful nibblers. There are many to choose from.

Apple slices (keep the skin on, it is beautiful)
Pineapple chunks
Cauliflower flowerettes
Radishes
Scallions
Carrots (watch content if you are close to your day's allowance)
Cherry tomatoes

DIP FOR FRUIT AND VEGETABLES

Mix 2 tablespoons low-sodium mayonnaise sprinkled with curry. Arrange vegetables and fruits the festive way. Pick leaves from your trees for a background; they are especially colorful in the fall. In the winter, use evergreens. If you don't have any trees, use parsley. You can buy a huge bouquet for 10 cents. Wash your parsley, drain, and keep in a covered jar or plastic bag in refrigerator. Parsley should not look "tired."

APPLE ROUNDS

An apple was Newton's friend when he was deciding all those theories. When an apple dropped on his head he wondered why it dropped straight down and not up, side-ways, or on a slant. He found out.

Slice unpared, cored apple, brush with lemon juice. Place on round of low-sodium bread the same size. Fill center with jam or peanut butter.

1 apple, 2 mg. sodium and 75 calories.

1 tablespoon lemon juice, negligible sodium and 4 calories.

1 tablespoon jam, 1 mg. sodium and 55 calories.

1 tablespoon low-sodium peanut butter, 7 mg. sodium and 100 calories.

ONION ROUNDS

Cut unsalted bread into squares or rounds. Place on each piece a thin slice of onion. Place 1 teaspoon of unsalty's mayonnaise on bread seasoned with dash of curry. Place canapés under broiler until piping hot. Serve at once. You may also use cucumbers in place of onions.

Each canapé, 4 mg. sodium and 53 calories.

TUNA FISH CANAPES

Flake canned low-sodium tuna fish with fork. Combine with sufficient low-sodium mayonnaise to make a good consistency to spread. Place on rounds of unsalty's bread. Add a dash of lemon juice, paprika, and chopped parsley. Heat under broiler, or serve cold.

½ cup canned low-sodium tuna, 31 mg. sodium and 122 calories.

1 tablespoon low-sodium mayonnaise, 6 mg. sodium and 92 calories.

DEVILED EGGS

4 hard-boiled eggs
1 tablespoon low-sodium mayonnaise
1 teaspoon tarragon vinegar
½ teaspoon mustard
¼ teaspoon chervil
¼ teaspoon rosemary
⅛ teaspoon cumin
Parsley
Paprika

Cut eggs in two, mash yolks, add other ingredients. Cream well. Fill eggs. Garnish with parsley and paprika.

4 SERVINGS. *Per serving, 70 mg. sodium and 100 calories.*

CURRIED AVOCADO DUNK

1 *mashed avocado*   2 *teaspoons vinegar*
¼ *teaspoon curry powder*

Cut avocado into halves lengthwise and remove seed and skin. Force fruit through sieve. Blend in curry and vinegar. Serve with unsalted melba toast or unsalted potato chips.

Total recipe, 6 mg. sodium and 486 calories.

Good Evening!

Try cardamom in your after-dinner coffee.

26 Some Parting "I Believe"

I BELIEVE that all our high schools and secondary schools should teach *each year* a compulsory course in basic nutrition and that our young men and women should understand FOOD FOR FITNESS. It isn't just the American hot dog and a soda pop.

I BELIEVE that our medical schools must have more courses in nutrition and present more facts concerning the elements which foods contain. The stomach is truly a miraculous organ—think of what it does for us 500 to 600 times a month!

I BELIEVE that the United States does not have to be the first country in the world in ratio of heart disease to population and that the heart, this machine, deserves more than equal time and energy spent in its care and feeding than the largest space machine. Wouldn't it be better to be first in our hearts than first in space? Then we might be first in both.

I BELIEVE that if you "Give to the world the best you have, the best will come back to you." Edward W. Bok wrote that to me when I was 12 years old. I wish I could always have followed these fine words.

I've enjoyed writing this book. It is my hope that it will be helpful.

27 Acknowledgments

Adele H. Colandrea   Helen B. Hauser

Millicent E. Colandrea   Sue F. Herkner

Mary Louise Cooper   Robert C. Notson

Rose G. Hafferberg   S. Richard Todd, Jr.

My wonderful Friends

28 Bibliography

American Heart Association Booklets: *Your 500 Milligrams Sodium Diet; Your 1000 Milligrams Sodium Diet; Your Mild Sodium-Restricted Diet.*

American Spice Trade Association Booklets: *A History of Spices; How to Use Spices; Spices.*

Alice V. Bradley, M.S., *Tables of Food Values.* Peoria, Ill.: Chas. A. Bennett Co., Inc., 1931.

Walter Kempner, M.D., *Radical Dietary Treatment of Hypertensive and Arteriosclerotic Vascular Disease, Heart and Kidney Disease, and Vascular Retinopathy.* Durham, N.C.: Duke University School of Medicine.

R. A. McCance and E. M. Widdowson, *The Chemical Composition of Foods.* Brooklyn, N.Y.: Chemical Publishing Co., 1947.

National Research Council, "Sodium-Restricted Diets," National Acad. of Sci. Publ. #32, July 1954.

Peterson, Skinner, Strong, *Elements of Food Biochemistry.* New York: Prentice-Hall, Inc., 1943.

Henry C. Sherman, Ph.D., Sc.D., *Chemistry of Food and Nutrition.* New York: The Macmillan Co., 1946.

Sodium and Potassium Analyses of Foods and Waters. Evansville, Ind.: Mead Johnson Research Laboratory, 1947.

Clara Mae Taylor, Ph.D., *Food Values in Shares and Weights.* 2nd Ed., New York: The Macmillan Co., 1959.

United States Department of Agriculture Handbook No. 8. Washington, D.C.

The Yearbook of Agriculture 1959. United States Department of Agriculture, Washington, D.C.

Index

ABOUT THE AUTHOR

ELMA W. BAGG wrote *COOKING WITHOUT A GRAIN OF SALT*—her first book—as a direct outgrowth of personal experience during years of experimentation and research. Mrs. Bagg lives with her husband in Millburn, New Jersey.

How's Your Health?

Bantam publishes a line of informative books, written by top experts to help you toward a healthier and happier life.